Walk With Me Through the Word

From Sin Unto Salvation

13 Week Bible Study

Walk With Me Through the Word; From Sin Unto Salvation
13 Week Bible Study
Bob Koonce Bible Studies Book 1

Unless otherwise identified, all scripture used are taken from the Authorized King James Version

ISBN - 9781080026418
Independently published

Nonfiction > Self-help > Spiritual
Nonfiction > Religion > Biblical Studies

Printed in the United States of America

Walk With Me Through the Word

From Sin Unto Salvation

13 Week Bible Study

Bishop Bob Koonce

Other Books and Bible Studies by Bishop Bob Koonce

Everyday Help for Everyday Christians – A 13 Week Bible Study

The Name Above Every Name; A Study of the Tetragrammaton

Visit the Corinthian Church; Commentary on 1 Corinthians

Visit the Corinthian Church Again; Commentary of 2 Corinthians

Understanding Revelation – Commentary of Revelation

The Man Called Peter-Commentaries to 1st and 2nd Peter

Beyond This Hill-A Christian Romance Novel

Earnestly Contending for the Faith-Jude's Commentary

Table of Contents

LESSON I: THE BATTLE FOR YOUR MIND

Lesson Focus: Since the devil must speak to our minds in order to damage our souls, we must retain control of all our mind all the time.

Scripture Selection:
I Timothy 4:1,2,6-8,13-16.

1 Now the Spirit speaketh expressly, that in the latter times some shall depart from the faith, giving heed to seducing spirits, and doctrines of devils;

2 Speaking lies in hypocrisy; having their conscience seared with a hot iron;

6 If thou put the brethren in remembrance of these things, thou shalt be a good minister of Jesus Christ, nourished up in the words of faith and of good doctrine, whereunto thou hast attained.

7 But refuse profane and old wives' fables and exercise thyself rather unto godliness.

8 For bodily exercise profiteth little: but godliness is profitable unto all things, having promise of the life that now is, and of that which is to come.

13 Till I come, give attendance to reading, to exhortation, to doctrine.

15 Meditate upon these things; give thyself wholly to them; that thy profiting may appear to all.

16 Take heed unto thyself, and unto the doctrine; continue in them: for in doing this thou shalt both save thyself, and them that hear thee.

I.   DOCTRINE NEEDS TO BE UNDERSTOOD.

The word doctrine comes from the Greek word didache, which means, "that which is taught." In our teaching we automatically use doctrine, therefore, it is very important that we know that our doctrine is founded on truth. Uncountable sums of teaching are not based on truth.

Like it or not, every person listens to **doctrine** constantly. Without it, sales would cease, production would stop, and a nation would sink to the lowest level of poverty. Everything and everyone about us promotes doctrine. (Our minds are constantly under some pressure to change, whether it be to purchase, sell or give something away.) Something is constantly trying to **teach** us, to indoctrinate us.

As long as a person is **satisfied** with a status quo, his/her mind can't be changed. It is the duty of the teacher to indoctrinate the student; to change a mind. As a rule, people don't make big decisions automatically. They take time to think: "What are they trying to put on me?" "What do I get out of this thing he/she/they are trying to manipulate me into?" "Why am I considering this?" These are just a few examples of things that run through people's minds. The "Why?" is probably the greatest obstacle to teaching that must be removed.

1

II. TEACHING HASN'T BEEN DONE UNTIL LEARNING OCCURS.

And that's quite a statement. Teaching isn't completed until learning occurs. Normal, non-incapacitated people possess these five senses:

1. Sight   3. Taste   5. Feel
2. Sound   4. Smell

Most of us normally use all five of these senses in our everyday living, and, usually, without our even taking notice of the fact. In using these senses, we need not only appreciate the fact that we possess them, but we should also realize that some of these senses are used more in the learning process than others.

While all five senses are important, those of **seeing** and of **hearing** are undoubtedly priceless. The other three senses: taste, feel, and smell depend almost totally on what we **see** or what we **hear**.

We would never be tempted to purchase something if we couldn't in some way **see** it. We would not buy an instrument that we couldn't **hear**. No one would taste food that he or she couldn't see, let alone feel, taste, or smell! I think you get the picture.

Now consider the effectiveness of sight and hearing in shaping behavioral patterns.

Our eyes contain much more learning power than do our brains. The learning power of the eye should have been listed first, since the eyes have more sensory nerves connected to the brain than do the ears.

III. THERE IS A TREMENDOUS IMPORTANCE OF AUDIO-VISUAL TRAINING,

Advertisers recognize the potent force of the two senses of seeing and hearing. No one buys either a Packard or a Stutz automobile anymore, and the reason is obvious; neither of these once-great cars are in production today. Their demise is not due to faulty workmanship but to inadequate salesmanship. The public was not properly **indoctrinated** to make it want these fine cars, and so they went out of business.

The political atmosphere of the world teaches us another very graphic lesson. Through the medium of audio-visual sales tools, peoples' minds all over the world have been changed.

In 1945, there was only one Communist nation - the Soviet Union. Mainland China fell to the Communists in 1949, but by that time most of Soviet-controlled Europe had come under the hammer and sickle. With China's fall, over half of the earth's population fell to the Red flag.

In 1946, approximately two thirds (2/3) of the world's nations were either democracies or democratically influenced. That compares to the 2000's figure of less than **1/3** of the earth's nations remaining democracies. **And the reason is obvious. That change** can be attributed to the **fact** that people have allowed themselves to be indoctrinated-their minds have been changed.

We need to understand how this was done.

Confucius say... A quote attributed to Confucius goes like this: "One picture is worth a thousand words." That may be true. What you see teaches you more than what you hear is fact, however. Television and the internet produce both **pictures** and **words**. What mighty tools for **indoctrination**!

Remember, you retain **much** more of what you **see** than what you hear. Newspapers and television, especially **television,** have been powerful allies to the forces that have changed our world. **And they're not done changing either!**

Totalitarian adherents (Communists and the like) have never changed their goals. Communism's goal has always been to gain control of the media, and by the media, gain control of people's minds. And it has worked!

The Communists' aim has never changed. Vladimir Lenin (the first Communist dictator of the Soviet Union) reportedly said, "Give me control of the alphabet, and I'll eventually control the world." Democracy-loving people must never be hoodwinked into thinking that Communism is dead or even sleeping. It is very much alive and just as aggressive as ever. Adolph Hitler reputedly said, "Tell a lie often enough and people will eventually believe it." Oh, the power of the media!

It's hard to teach old dogs new tricks. Satan knows this; the Communists and other totalitarians know this, so they use the media to pound, pound, pound their agenda into people's minds. Just think of what this does to a child's developing mind. And that's why there's such an onslaught on youth of today. How great is the enemy's grip on the young? If the enemy can gain control of children, it most certainly will dictate their actions as adults. Consider the next point in this lesson carefully.

IV. THE AVERAGE AMERICAN CHILD WATCHES 28 HOURS OF T.V. WEEKLY.

If ever the odds were stacked against society, we certainly must be witnessing it now when statistics tell us that the average (not spoiled, pampered, but average) child in America watches television 28 hours a week. That's only 12 hours less than the average American worker spends on the job! Incredulous! And that is the beginning only of the sad saga that the media plays in children's lives. A 2006 report by Citizens for Independent Public Broadcasting (CIPB), Pittsburgh, PA, provided the ensuing figures:

Television is pumped into the average American home an average of 7 hours and 40 minutes, just 20 minutes short of eight hours a day. Over half (53 percent) of children from ages 6-17 have televisions in their bedrooms. Over half (58 percent) have television on during mealtimes. The average youth watches **1,023** hours of TV per year, while going to school **900** hours - **123** hours less than spent watching TV. Guess which has the most effect.

Television is pumped into millions of homes daily for one specific purpose - to **sell** something. **Ninety percent** of Saturday morning ads promote sugary cereals, candy bars, salty canned foods, and other junk foods. Put the right picture on a box and rev up the presentation of the ad, children become easy targets. Never under-estimate the influence of children when they become sold on something. There will always be some version or another of "snack, crack, and pop." Cereal and junk food merchants will see to that.

Children spend a staggering 28 **billion** of their own money yearly toward purchases. The business sector wants that money, of course, so it advertises heavily on TV. **Six thousand** commercials parade to the front of the silver screen. Children account for 600 **billion** dollars of their parents' spending. Think of it!

But are the commercial ads the end for the selling power of TV? More alarming by far than luring a child to buy junk foods, etc., is the fact that television has become increasingly infested with violence, depictions of horror, murder, rape, and on and on. Before the end of elementary school, television children will be bombarded with **100,000** acts of violence - **8,000** of them murders. By the age of 18, **40,000** murders, many of them quite gory, will have flashed across the TV screen.

REAL VISION, Facts and Figures, of TV-Turnoff, Washington, DC, Autumn, 2007, lists figures that should concern parents, and everybody else, for that matter:

Children watching television are barraged with **40,000** ads a year. As alarming as this figure may seem, consider this about children: Brand loyalty can be imbedded in a child's mind as early as age two. What if a loyalty is formed by violent or lurid movies that unsuspecting or uncaring parents didn't prevent the baby from watching? The "sales" effected by ads is in no way restricted to children, of course, but little minds are tender and there for the making. **Ninety seven percent** of children under six have products based on characters from TV shows or movies.

Ninety nine percent of families with children 0-6 of age have at least one television. A 2003 figure showed that **50** percent of American homes had **3** or more television sets. Pathetically, the TV set has become the **babysitter** for an alarming percentage of America's children. **Forty five** percent of this nation's parents admit that they let their TVs entertain their children when they have something more important to do. Whatever could there be more important than watching one's own child?

Now, how much time does religion, any religion, have to combat this tremendous infusion into children's brains?
1. Normally, a child spends less than **one(1)** hour in Sunday School weekly.
2. How much of that 1 hour does the child retain to shape its character?

Contrast the 28 hours of television, not to mention the internet, with the 1 hour of religious education offered outside the home. A Sunday School teacher **might** get to teach a child **45 minutes** each week. (Many children don't attend church every week, so there is a loss there.) Children will retain less than 1/3 as much of what the teacher **tells** them over what they **saw** on television. If children actually retain 10% of what has been taught during 45 minutes of teaching, only 4.5 minutes of religious education must combat all the other stuff that the poor, immature minds have been bombarded with during the 28 hours of television alone. What a tremendous imbalance!

V. ARE YOU IN CONTROL OF YOUR OWN MIND?

That's a great question - a loaded one at that. Be honest with yourself, also, when considering the following questions. You don't have to share your answers, but you certainly must live with them, whether spoken orally or not. And what does a person do with a mind that condemns the very person that owns it? Good question. Are you in total control of your own mind? Perhaps you could be better equipped to assess your own condition after answering the following questions.

1. How much time do you spend hearing, reading, and meditating on the Word of God?
2. How much time do you allot the media to shape your mind?
3. Do you know that televisions run **7 hours, forty minutes** a day in the <u>average</u> American home?

REAL VISION further reported that the average adult in America watches **4 hours of TV** <u>daily</u>. **Ninety nine percent** of U.S. families have at least one TV in their homes. **99 percent!** That's almost astounding! Well, are we to live in the dark ages and not possess a television, a computer, or some other electronic instrument? No, that's not the point at all. Seriously ponder the following paragraph.

50 percent (½) of American families own **3 or more** TVs. **40 percent** often or always watch TV while eating dinner. **49 percent**, just under half, say they watch too much TV. Now, why would they admit to something like that if they didn't feel they were too heavily influenced by the programming they've heaped upon themselves? **55** percent of young adults say they put off their bedtime for the **internet**. The battle for the mind is on in this world!

The media of television, radio, computers with internet capabilities, radio, newspapers, telephones, and all types of new devices emerging on the market, steadily battle for your mind. Cell phones, Mp3 players, cruel and wicked video "games" for the computer, My Space, and so many other wonders of this electronic age are out there in front of all of us. Are you capable of retaining complete control of your own thinking in the face of this tremendous attack?

The onslaught for the minds of children and young adults is not restricted to that age group, as you can surmise from the foregoing information. No one is inoculated against the media' onslaught for control of minds, however. A great percentage of adults in America work an 8-hour job, yet still spend an incredible amount of time before a T.V. or computer. Those not employed may be even greater targets for the media, being longer exposed to T.V. or the Internet.

It has probably taken very little of your time to read through this entire lesson, but your mind has been affected. You've drawn conclusions. You've made decisions. You've been changed, if ever so slightly. You may be shocked or disgusted, but you have been changed, nevertheless, and hopefully for the wiser. Wherever you are, be always reminded that something or someone is constantly trying to change you. Is the change good? Ask God for wisdom and strength to resist if it isn't.

At this very moment, are you yielding to something that you could well wish that you could undo a few years hence? Your spouse? Your children? Someone or something else? The battle is on; never allow anything to **corrupt** your mind. *And be not conformed to this world: but be ye transformed by the **renewing** of your **mind**, that ye may prove what is that good, and acceptable, and perfect will of God"* (Romans 12:2).

Editor's Note: Since this article was originally authored, some new developments have arrived to grab the attention of our little children, teens, young adults and of course, us! The computer has morphed itself into different sizes and shapes as to be available everywhere, but it comes with built in attention grabbers as they have become so large and so fast that , while they are wonderful for business, they also are amazingly adaptive at 'gaming.' Games for our young men and women are amazingly accurate in details; they are fast enough to handle almost real time action and they are horribly addictive. Our youth are so absorbed in the gaming action, they are less and less involved with family and their former activities, whether one is a parent, the children are ignored; if teenagers, their parents have difficulty getting them to the supper table.

The telephone, you know that piece of equipment attached with a cord to the wall, and you used it to call friends, neighbors and bosses with? This little device has become the world's number 1 victor in the battle for our minds. Look around, everywhere you look, someone is looking at their phone playing some sort of a game or involved in many other of the actions the telephone (Cell) has morphed into. It is a phone, a computer, a calendar, a calculator, music player, typewriter, gamer and so much more. It is a one in a million-entertainment center. I added this not to take away from this excellent lesson, but to help you understand that as time moves on, so do satan's tactics. It's the same war, he just uses different weapons.

LESSON II: HE'S ALIVE!

Lesson Focus: Three men died on Golgotha two thousand years ago; two of them are still dead. A resurrected Christ is **fact**. Every person, therefore, will give answer before Him for deeds done in this life.

Scripture Selection:

Revelation 1:11-18

11 Saying, I am Alpha and Omega, the first and the last: and What thou seest, write in a book, and send it unto the seven churches which are in Asia; unto Ephesus, and unto Smyrna, and unto Pergamos, and unto Thyatira, and unto Sardis, and unto Philadelphia, and unto Laodicea.

12 And I turned to see the voice that spake with me. And being turned, I saw seven golden candlesticks;;

13 And in the midst of the seven candlesticks (one) like unto the Son of man, clothed with a garment down to the foot, and girt about the paps with a golden girdle.

14 His head and his hairs (were) white like wool, as white as snow; and his eyes (were) as a flame of fire;

15 And his feet like unto fine brass, as if they burned in a furnace; and his voice as the sound of many waters.

16 And he had in his right hand seven stars: and out of his mouth went a sharp two edged sword: and his countenance (was) as the sun shineth in his strength.

17 And when I saw him I fell at his feet (as) dead. And he laid his right hand upon me, saying unto me, Fear not; I am the first and the last:

18 I (am) he that liveth, and (was) dead; and, behold, I am alive for evermore, Amen; and have the keys of hell and of death.

I. A CHRISTIAN IS PROOF OF JESUS' RESURRECTION.

Jesus Christ carried no sword, commanded no army, wrote no books, and built no edifices, yet He today commands a greater army than **all** the military rulers of all time **combined**! He disdained the use of force, commanded His disciple Peter to dispose his sword, and yet He commands a mighty army of believers to this day. Men and women surrender and kneel before Him, despite the fact He died nearly two thousand years ago. And the reason for this homage is Jesus Christ is risen from a death He endured for the sins of all mankind.

Three men, Jesus Christ and two thieves, died on crosses two thousand years ago. Our Savior only has risen from the dead. The other two crucified with Him are still dead and await judgment before the resurrected One, Christ Jesus. Earth's multitudes, past and present, will also be judged by Him.

7

Many of the notables of the world have lived and died, but none of them exercise power **from within** in their followers. Obedience to their teachings is often enforced by external pressure. Many years ago, a Sikh described his religion to the church of which I was the pastor. He stated, without any sign of compunction, that he carried a dagger on his hip. When asked why he carried the weapon, he bluntly stated, "We carry knives to dispatch those that are unworthy to live," meaning anyone not of his faith. Similar methods are practiced by other false religions.

The Law of Moses demands obedience, but gives no power to overcome evil. The apostle Paul plainly declared that the Law failed because of the weakness of men. Its precepts are good, but the Law was not designed to save, but to bring an awareness of sin. There is nothing in the Law that provides resurrection power. That power can come through the Lord Jesus Christ only.

Buddhism demands conformity to its ritualistic worship, but supplies no power to overcome sin.

Hinduism embraces all sorts of discrepancies, such as pampering sacred monkeys in the temples and sacred cows on the streets, oftentimes while the poor go hungry.

Driven from his hometown of Mecca, **Mohammed** fled to Medina, returned a few years later with his followers, captured Mecca, and subjugated all there to Islam , his new religion, and to the worship of Allah. From there, **Islam** swept the mid-eastern world, and for a time threatened to conquer all of Europe. And the conquering was done with the fanatic's sword. Islam is maintained by that same force today. There is no **resurrection** power in Islam. Mohammed has not been seen alive since his death in 632 A.D.

Of all the religions in the world, **Jesus Christ**, the Cornerstone of Christianity, is the **only** one to have appeared alive again after His death. That's resurrection power vividly displayed!

II. THE PROPHETS IN THE OLD TESTAMENT WEREN'T WRONG.

And you will see from the following examples that their prophecies weren't guesses but actual revelations of occurrences that would not literally take place for hundreds, even thousands of years after they were uttered.

Abraham, who was born 2,165 years before Christ, uttered a potent prophecy on Mt. Moriah concerning the coming of the Messiah and the Messiah's becoming the sacrifice for sin.

And Isaac spake unto Abraham his father, and said, My father: and he said, Here am I, my son. And he said, Behold the fire and the wood: but where is the lamb for a burnt offering? [8] And Abraham said, My son, God will provide himself a lamb for a burnt offering: so they went both of them together. (Genesis 22:7-8)

1,400 years before Christ, **Moses** prophesied: *The Lord thy God will raise up unto thee a Prophet from the midst of thee, of thy brethren, like unto me; unto him ye shall hearken;* (Deut. 18:15)

Almost **1,000** years before Christ, King David prophetically spoke of the definite resurrection of Jesus Christ. *For thou wilt not leave my soul in hell; neither wilt thou suffer thine Holy One to see corruption.* (Psalm 16:10)

Over **700** years before Christ, Isaiah told of the Messiah's coming. *For unto us a child is born, unto us a son is given: and the government shall be upon his shoulder: and his name shall be called Wonderful, Counsellor, The mighty God, The everlasting Father, The Prince of Peace.* (Isaiah 9:6)

700 years before Christ, Micah, a contemporary of Isaiah, foretold the actual birthplace of the Messiah. *But thou, Bethlehem Ephratah, though thou be little among the thousands of Judah, yet out of thee shall he come forth unto me that is to be ruler in Israel; whose goings forth have been from of old, from everlasting.* (Micah 5:2) Micah's prophecy was so accurate that King Herod knew the exact birthplace of the Messiah. Herod was afraid that the Messiah would replace his throne, so he ordered all the male babies at Bethlehem under two years old to be killed.

Now...since every one of the prophecies happened <u>exactly</u> the way the prophets said they would, and all those prophets were **Bible** writers, then one can only conclude that the **Bible is true**. And since the **Bible is true**, and since that same **Bible** declares that Jesus Christ died and rose from the dead never to die again - Jesus Christ's resurrection is **fact**. Can any other religion make the same claim?

III. THE ABSENCE OF JESUS' CORPSE SPEAKS VOLUMES.
And how! The Jewish leaders couldn't produce a corpse to prove that Jesus was still dead, so they bought off the men who stood guard over the sepulcher and gave them assurance that they would not be punished for dereliction of duty. Their motive was plain for all to see. They knew that Jesus had resurrected; otherwise, they wouldn't have bought off the guards. They would simply have ridiculed anyone who said that Jesus was alive.

A living Jesus, in their minds, posed a threat to their occupations. Since the High Priest was the virtual ruler of the Jews, a new King would displace him and those associated with him. That they would not allow. This is not to say that all Jews are bad, just as all Gentiles aren't, but some Jews were and are bad, just as there were and are bad Gentiles also. The ruling Jews at the time of Jesus' passion were so corrupt that the death of an innocent man seemed to mean nothing at all to them.

IV. JOSEPHUS, IN HIS ANTIQUITIES OF THE JEWS, WROTE...
"Now there was about this time, Jesus, a wise man, if it be lawful to call him a man, for he was a doer of wonderful works, a teacher of such men as receive the truth with pleasure. He drew over to him both many of the Jews and many of the gentiles. He was the Christ and when Pilate, at the

suggestion of the principal men amongst us, had condemned him to the cross, those that loved him at the first did not forsake him. For he appeared alive again the third day, as the divine prophets had foretold these and ten thousand other wonderful things concerning him; and the tribe of Christians, so named from him, are not extinct to this day."

V. SECULAR SCHOLARS AFFIRM THE AUTHENTICITY OF THE BIBLE; THUS, THEY ALSO AFFIRM THE RESURRECTION OF JESUS CHRIST.

One of the most important Roman historians is Tacitus. In 115 A.D. he recorded Nero's persecution of the Christians, in the process of which he wrote the following: "Christus, from whom the name had its origin, suffered the extreme penalty during the reign of Tiberius at the hands of one of our procurators, Pontius Pilatus, and a most mischievous superstition, thus checked for the moment, again broke out not only in Judea, . . . but even in Rome."

"The "superstition" to which Tacitus referred was Christianity, of course, and he called it not only a superstition but a 'most mischievous superstition.'" Something, in his mind, was again exclaiming Christianity throughout the Roman Empire. Could that force have been a living Christ and not just the memory of Him? Of course it was.

Archeology continues to verify the accuracy of the Gospels, and all four Gospels tell of the resurrection of Jesus. The names of many of the Israelite cities, events, and people described in them have now been located. All the discoveries made are consistent with the details in the crucifixion account given by the writers of the Gospels. These facts lend indirect support for the biblical accounts of Jesus' crucifixion and that the tomb was empty.

At one time, scholars did not view Luke's historical accounts in his Gospel and Acts as accurate. There appeared to be no evidence for several cities, persons, and locations that Luke named in his works. However, archaeological advances have revealed that Luke was a very accurate historian and the two books he authored remain accurate documents of history.

One of the greatest archaeologists is the late Sir William Ramsay. He studied under one of the famous liberal German historical schools in the mid-nineteenth century. Known for its scholarship, this school taught that the New Testament was not a historical document. With that premise, Ramsay investigated biblical claims as he searched through Asia Minor. What he discovered caused him to reverse his initial view. The following quote is Ramsay's assessment of Luke:

"I began with a mind unfavorable to it [Acts], for the ingenuity and apparent completeness of the Tubingen theory had at one time quite convinced me. It did not then in my line of life to investigate the subject minutely; but more recently I found myself often brought into contact with the Book of Acts as an authority for the topography, antiquities, and society of Asia Minor. It was gradually borne in upon me that in various details the narrative showed marvelous truth."

10

After thirty years of study, Ramsay concluded,

"Luke is a historian of first rank; not merely are his statements of facts trustworthy...this author should be placed along with the very greatest of historians."

It is that very Luke, who, in his Gospel of St. Luke, described the resurrection of Jesus so vividly and recorded, also, several of His appearances to His followers.

The **resurrection** of **Jesus Christ** is the backbone truth of Christianity. Without that fact, Christianity would be no different than any other religion - but Jesus lives. Many secular scholars have attacked the resurrection account, only to find themselves converted by the truth of their research. Dr. Simon Greenleaf, founder of the Harvard Law School, noted:

"Propagating this new faith, even in the most inoffensive and peaceful manner, [early Christians received] contempt, opposition... and cruel deaths. Yet this faith they zealously did propagate, and all these miseries they endured undismayed, nay rejoicing. As one after another was put to a miserable death, the survivors only [continued] their work with increased vigor and resolution... The annals of military warfare afford scarcely an example of like heroic constancy, patience, and unblenching courage... If it were morally possible for them to have been deceived in this matter, every human motive operated to lead them to discover and avow their error. From these [considerations] there is no escape but in the perfect conviction and admission that they were good men, testifying to that which they had carefully observed...and well knew to be true."

Dr. Greenleaf is considered by many to have been one of the greatest legal minds we have had in the U.S. He was formerly an outspoken skeptic of Christianity and who set out to disprove the deity of Christ. In the end he concluded that the **Resurrection** was true "beyond any reasonable doubt." Greenleaf became a Christian after studying the evidence for himself. Many top legal minds agree with Greenleaf that if the case for Christ's death and resurrection were taken to a court of law, it would undoubtedly win. The claims are very well established and verified by independent and converging proofs.

VI. NO TOMB ANYWHERE COULD PERMANENTLY HAVE HELD OUR LORD. Maggots were denied a meal on Jesus' body. In Psalms 16:10, David prophesied of Jesus saying, *"For thou wilt not leave my soul in hell* (the grave); *neither wilt thou suffer thine Holy One to see corruption"* (decay; rot). David also said that it was impossible that He (Jesus) be holden (captured and controlled) by death. *Whom God hath raised up, having loosed the pains of death: because it was not possible that he should be holden of it.* (Acts 2:24) Sealed behind a huge stone and guarded by elite soldiers, Jesus rose from the grave without ever disturbing their stone! After He had risen from the dead, an angel rolled the stone from the door of the sepulcher, not to allow the Lord out, but to enable His followers to get in!

VII. THE FOLLOWING IS POSITIVE PROOF THAT JESUS CHRIST IS RISEN.

At this very instant Jesus Christ stands ready to deliver the drunkard, the sex deviate, the drug addict, the murderer, the harlot, and perhaps greater still---the dead religionist. Millions still witness the power of a living, resurrected Christ. Tears still flow in conviction and tongues still sing the praises of a living Christ. The David Wilkersons of personal evangelism still dare to venture into the ghettoes and convert the Nicky Cruz's with the marvelous message, "He is not here! He is risen!"

How about you, dear reader? Have you experienced the saving grace of a wonderful, loving, living Lord? Would you like to? Bow your head, get on your knees if possible, and simply tell Jesus that you want to unload your sin, mean what you say, and ask Him to forgive you. Tell someone else about how wonderful it feels after you've repented.

LESSON III: GOD HATES SIN

Lesson Focus: Sin is the complete opposite of God. It denies that He is Almighty. There can never be a truce between sin and a sinless God. One of these forces will eventually be annihilated, and the One remaining certainly won't be sin!

Scripture Selection: Romans 7:5,7-9,11,14,17,24; 8:32.

5For when we were in the flesh, the motions of sins, which were by the law, did work in our members to bring forth fruit unto death.

7What shall we say then? Is the law sin? God forbid. Nay, I had not known sin, but by the law: for I had not known lust, except the law had said, Thou shalt not covet.

8 But sin, taking occasion by the commandment, wrought in me all manner of concupiscence. For without the law sin was dead.

9 For I was alive without the law once: but when the commandment came, sin revived, and I died.

11 For sin, taking occasion by the commandment, deceived me, and by it slew me.

14 For we know that the law is spiritual: but I am carnal, sold under sin.

17 Now then it is no more I that do it, but sin that dwelleth in me.

24 O wretched man that I am! who shall deliver me from the body of this death?

8:32 He that spared not his own Son, but delivered him up for us all, how shall he not with him also freely give us all things?

I. SIN, WHAT IS IT?

Actually, no long definition is needed to describe sin. We all feel its effect on our lives, we've all performed it, felt guilty over it, repented of it, or glazed our minds over in an effort to insulate our consciences against it. Sin and a guiltless conscience will not fit under the same hat. Good and bad mix no better than oil and water. Sin is diametrically opposed to Godliness. The etymology (history) of the word *sin* traces back to Middle English *sinne*, then to Old English *sunta*. *Sunta* is akin to High German *sunta sin*. From there the trail fades into seeming oblivion, yet the word began somewhere in some language. A definite demarcation line for righteousness vs. evil seems to have been drawn on a permanent basis by the patriarch, Abraham. Paleo (ancient) Hebrew for the word would not have been written or enunciated the same way it is done in English, of course, but the sense of the word would not have changed. It is reasonable to assume that the Wilderness of *Sin* and the word *sin* have been translated through the ages from a common background. It is entirely possible that a name for evil began with Abraham, and that his chosen word has been preserved and transliterated through the centuries into its present form. Abraham may actually have coined the word.

Abraham is the only recorded monotheist (believer in one God only) of his time in Bible history. The patriarch was so closely akin to God that he was rightly called *the friend of God*. Abraham knew God, and God certainly knew Abraham. Abraham knew for a certainty that the worship, practices, and the oblations offered to the heathen moon god *sin* absolutely were an affront to his God. All the things, then, that Abraham knew were noxious to God could have become known as sin.

God would never sin, because it is anti-nature to Him. A tree is a near-perfect example to portray God. Allow a man with an axe to cut on a tree and he will chop the same type of wood all the way through. Once the tree is felled, the axe-wielder can hew lengthwise or crosswise and continue to chop until the tree is pure sawdust, but the smallest chip from that tree will be the same type of wood as was the tree from whence it was hewn. And so it is with God. He is the same through and through. He will oppose anything that is foreign to His nature. Notice again the tree.

Any foreign material driven into a tree, such as a nail, becomes an instant enemy. The tree will do its utmost to surround and absorb the intruder if it can't expel it someway. And as long as it lives, it will despise that intruding nail! There can never be a truce between God and sin.

And though transgression against God, that today we call sin, may have received its title from Abraham, but evil or sin existed long before Abraham. Look at Scripture found in Isaiah 14:12-15:

12How art thou fallen from heaven, O lucifer, son of the morning! how art thou cut down to the ground, which didst weaken the nations! 13For thou hast said in thine heart, I will ascend into heaven, I will exalt my throne above the stars of God: I will sit also upon the mount of the congregation, in the sides of the north: 14I will ascend above the heights of the clouds: I will be like the most High. 15Yet thou shalt be brought down to hell, to the sides of the pit.

II. SIN ORIGINATED IN HEAVEN, BUT IT WASN'T TOLERATED THERE.

Not for a moment! In the presence of the indescribable beauty of Paradise, Lucifer (Satan, the devil) became utterly intoxicated with his own beauty. He hated his Maker (still does), enticed vain angels into a confederacy with him, and attempted to set up his own kingdom. He imagined himself on a par with God, a position that could not be, and a lesson the devil was ultimately to learn. The prophet, Isaiah, gave us an actual account of the incident.

Isaiah 14:12-15 How art thou fallen from heaven, O lucifer, son of the morning! how art thou cut down to the ground, which didst weaken the nations! 13For thou hast said in thine heart, I will ascend into heaven, I will exalt my throne above the stars of God: I will sit also upon the mount of the congregation, in the sides of the north: 14I will ascend above the heights of the clouds: I will be like the most High. ¹⁵*Yet thou shalt be brought down to hell, to the sides of the pit.*

God created living things, never robots. He endowed every creature with a choice. And in the light of the fact that angelic beings are so superior to man, the fall of Satan because of pride is an appalling thing.

God doesn't want robotic, mechanical praise. He doesn't want wind-up toys to simply mouth prerecorded messages. Humans have the choice to accept or shun Him. The devil chose to reject Him. Satan looked upon his own beauty and splendor, then viewed the glory of God with lust rather than awe, and actually tried to displace God. Had he been allowed to remain in glory, heaven would have ceased to be holy.

There is but one supreme being. There can never be more than one Supreme. With a Supreme, how could there be another? Satan didn't seek to <u>replace</u>, but to <u>displace</u> God. He didn't want to be what God is; he wanted to be himself in the position of God.

Everything that God is not, the devil is. Where God is love, the devil is the epitome of hate and everything that corresponds to it. We understand things by contrasts. We understand heat by cold, comfort by discomfort, etc. What a contrast to God Satan offers!

III. SIN EVENTUALLY ALWAYS BRINGS TRAUMATIC CONSEQUENCES.

The Bible is full of examples, and though only five subjects are listed in this lesson, there are many more that could here be presented from and in addition to the Bible accounts. Visit morgues, hospitals, jails; view so many around you whose luck has run out; it won't be hard to get the picture. But since the Bible is so accurate and complete, we'll consider some examples from it.

Adam and Eve, the first humans to inhabit Earth, yielded to their lust to explore the forbidden and forfeited their right to inhabit the earthly paradise of the Garden of Eden. We've all said or heard, "I just wish I could get my hands on Adam!" Adam made one mistake. How about you?

Situated in a utopia where everything was perfect - perfect climate, no rain, yet every plant and creature in a perfect state. No death, so there was no aging. Imagine! No death, so no aches or sickness. No 3-meal days; there was plenty of food and they could eat any time they wanted. No worries about being attacked by gnats, ants, flies, or West-Nile mosquitoes. No worry about being attacked by wild beasts. Animals, insects, reptiles, plants, and birds had not yet been geared to kill. They were fitted for that after Adam's fall. And for just one bite of the forbidden fruit, they lost it all!

Cain, the first human to be born on earth, exhibited mankind's rebellious nature. He knew full well that offering vegetables and fruit to God was no sacrifice at all. There was no sacrifice in his giving, because he could grow more. He wouldn't have been pleased if he, himself, had been presented with vegetables and fruits that he already had more of than he knew what to do with. He didn't give anything he couldn't replace. He didn't make a sacrifice; he offered a substitute, but consider his brother, Abel.

Abel offered an animal from his flock as a sacrifice to God. He offered the life of an animal, a life he could not replace. Cain became murderously angry because he knew Abel's offering was a sacrifice to God and his own offering was an insult. His wrath drove him to murder his brother and then suffer the judgment of God by being driven from civilization to roam a hostile world by himself. Sin comes with a high price tag.

Sodom and Gomorrah are the names of two ancient cities that the bulk of which many people of this world have probably never heard. Many of the guided tours to Israel include a tour of the wasted, salty area near and around the Dead Sea that is believed by many to be the site of these two cities. In fact, tourists are told that one of the many salt pillars there could actually be Lot's disobedient wife.

Not only were the two cities, Sodom and Gomorrah destroyed, but the whole area that encompassed those two cities. What terrible, awful sin could have compelled God to destroy all that area with a perpetual destruction? The consequences of homosexuality are horrific.

Homosexuality is a sin in God's face. It contradicts His Word: *And Adam said, This is now bone of my bones, and flesh of my flesh: she shall be called Woman, because she was taken out of Man. [24] Therefore shall a man leave his father and his mother, and shall cleave unto his wife: and they shall be one flesh* (Genesis 2:23, 24). God's command, first to Adam and Eve, to be fruitful and multiply and fill the world could hardly be carried out with homosexual unions. Aids is but one of the consequences of this terrible sin - God's impending wrath is quite another.

Sin on a wholesale level caused all land-dwelling creatures, including and, especially, all mankind to be destroyed by a calamitous, whole-earth flood. The Bible describes the state of all mankind prior to the Flood as "...that the wickedness of man was great in the earth, and that every imagination of the thoughts of his heart was only evil continually" Gen. 6:5. There is also compelling evidence in fossil beds and sea creatures' fossils found in rocks far, far above sea level that the Flood also destroyed large amounts of sea life as well. And this terrible judgment was brought about as a punishment for <u>sin!</u>

IV. NOW NOTICE THE NATURE OF SIN.
Then when lust hath conceived, it bringeth forth sin: and sin, when it is finished, bringeth forth death (James 1:15).

James 1:15 describes the situation pretty accurately - when lust is conceived (taken into one's heart) it produces sin. The end-result for sin is <u>death</u>, the <u>supreme</u> <u>penalty</u> for any capital offense.

Why would anyone in his or her right mind ever succumb to something so terrible as sin? The fact of the matter is that we all have yielded to this terrible beast of a slave master. The one that kills!

IV.   SIN DEMANDS PAYMENT, THUS...

There is a definite need for a propitiation (pronounced "pro-pish-e-a-shun") meaning "a bloody covering" in the minds of many scholars. Merriam-Webster's dictionary defines propitiation as "something that takes the place of," which certainly describes the role of our Redeemer, Jesus Christ.

Sin demands payment; every soul on earth needs a propitiation, a bloody covering. It is absolutely essential that everyone remember that sin carries the price tag of death! Someone had to die for our sin since we can't resurrect from the grave on our own, having paid the penalty that sin demands. Someone has to become our bloody covering. Jesus Christ can wondrously fill that need.

V. WHO IS GUILTY?

Everyone! That's such a simple question to answer. Everyone has, and most people still do. No man or woman has ever lived who has not sinned, with the exception of Jesus Christ. This is why we stand guilty before the sinless One. Romans 3:23 states it as it is: *For all have sinned, and come short of the glory of God*. And as Romans 3:10 states it: *As it is written, There is none righteous, no, not one:* That includes everyone without forgiveness from God, and this is why Jesus Christ, the sinless One, is the only One Who can and will come to our rescue.

VI.   PERHAPS YOU'RE ASKING, "WHAT MUST I DO?"

The first, most important essential for repentance is Godly sorrow. A person must see himself for what he is - burdened with sin, filthy with sin, spiritually dead in sin, without God in sin,- and then realize that he cannot help himself. In his grief over his helpless situation, the wise person will turn to God in supplication. It is then and only then that God can and will help him.

Repentance is not salvation completed, and it is heresy to proclaim such a doctrine. But repentance is important, necessary, and it brings such a feeling of relief to a weary soul, because the burden of transgression has been laid out before God, and the sinner has admitted guilt in the words, "I'm sorry. Please forgive me." At that moment of sincerity, the sinner is no longer an enemy of God because of repentance, which literally means "to turn around."

In our next lesson we'll explain the difference between mere repentance and full Bible salvation. But for the moment, do it because it is the right thing to do if you know that you are not at peace with God. And we won't desert you in this quest either. We've prayed sincerely over this lesson, so know that we unite with you in prayer as you bow your head to God in prayer in seeking Him. Wouldn't you love to give it a try? Right now?

LESSON IV: REPENT

Lesson Focus: It is extremely important to show the difference between the joy that comes with repentance and the assurance of salvation through obedience to the Word.

Scripture Selection: Matt. 3:2, 4:17; Mark 1:15; Luke 13:1,2,5; Acts 2:38, 3:19, 17:30, 26:20.

Matt. 3:2 And saying, Repent ye: for the kingdom of heaven is at hand.

Matt. 4:17 From that time Jesus began to preach, and to say, Repent: for the kingdom of heaven is at hand.

Mark 1:15 And saying, The time is fulfilled, and the kingdom of God is at hand: repent ye, and believe the gospel.

Luke 13:1 There were present at that season some that told him of the Galileans, whose blood Pilate had mingled with their sacrifices.

2 And Jesus answering said unto them, Suppose ye that these Galileans were sinners above all the Galileans, because they suffered such things?

5 I tell you, Nay: but, except ye repent, ye shall all likewise perish.

Acts 2:38 Then Peter said unto them, Repent, and be baptized every one of you in the name of Jesus Christ for the remission of sins, and ye shall receive the gift of the Holy Ghost.

3:19 Repent ye therefore, and be converted, that your sins may be blotted out, when the times of refreshing shall come from the presence of the Lord;

17:30 And the times of this ignorance God winked at; but now commandeth all men every where to repent:

26:20 But showed first unto them of Damascus, and at Jerusalem, and throughout all the coasts of Judaea, and then to the Gentiles, that they should repent and turn to God, and do works meet for repentance.

The word "repent" is taken from the Greek verbs "metanoe" and "metamelomar". Meta, meaning, "after, and implying change" and noeo, meaning, "to perceive" definitely implies the overall definition of "to change one's mind afterwards." Our English word repent comes from the Latin re (again) plus poenitere (punishment). U.S. marines have used the word repent to mean, "to halt, turn around, and proceed the opposite direction from what they were headed originally." This would appear to be the most correct interpretation of what the Bible intends when it commands repentance.

Repent appears 9 times in Luke, 5 times in Acts, 12 times in Revelation, plus appearances in the other Gospels. It was the first word used by both John Baptist and Jesus Christ when they began their ministries. *"Repent for the Kingdom of God is at hand,"* was uttered by both of them. God places special emphasis on <u>turning around</u>, or <u>repentance</u>.

19

I. REPENTANCE IS BECAUSE OF SOMETHING.

Repentance is essential in a soul's quest for God. *Repent ye; for the kingdom of heaven is at hand* (Matthew 9:12). John the Baptist's central theme was repentance - a literal turning around and heading the opposite direction.

Repentance is the first step for anyone to take in approaching God, since we were all originally headed in the wrong direction. Repentance is always necessary because of something. We must turn around because we are headed in a direction away from the Kingdom of God. The Gospels, as well as other Books of the Bible, further inform us that dire circumstances await the person who persists in walking away from God and who will not repent or turn around!

As wonderful and as thrilling as the clean, pure feeling that we experience when we repent is, it is not salvation in itself, that is, all alone. It is simply and honestly only the first step in the process of salvation. Without further obedience to the Word of God, a person could and would ultimately be lost despite the fact that he once repented.

Our Lord Jesus Christ affirmed John Baptist's call for repentance. *Repent ye; for the kingdom of heaven is at hand* (Matthew 4:17) If there could be such a thing as a sinless being, then there would be no need for repentance. This has never been the case, nor will it ever be. All have sinned, so all must repent. *For all have sinned, and come short of the glory of God;* (Romans 3:23)

II. JESUS CONFIRMED JOHN THE BAPTIST' MESSAGE OF REPENTANCE.

The Scriptures all agree in all points and in every area. John Baptist and Jesus Christ gave identical commands on the subject of repentance. There is another subject linked here also that is too important to simply pass over, however, and that is the fact that God confirms every Bible truth with more than one witness. Here are two Scriptures that confirm this statement.

Matthew 18:16*But if he will not hear {thee},{then} take with thee one or two more, that in the mouth of two or three witnesses every word may be established.*

II Corinthians 13:1*This {is} the third {time} I am coming to you. In the mouth of two or three witnesses shall every word be established.*

God is not afraid that His Word be checked; He demands it! Bible truths, such as the need for repentance, are so important that the Lord didn't risk its misinterpretation with only a single Scripture to affirm it.

Jesus preached that without repentance everyone would perish. ....*Jesus answering said unto them, Suppose ye that these Galileans were sinners above all the Galileans, because they suffered such things? ³I tell you, Nay: but, except ye repent, ye shall all likewise perish* (Luke 13:2,3).

Whether we admit our sin or hide under a cloak of self-righteousness, everyone must repent. And that is for a reason, the reason being that all, everyone has sinned, so all must repent. *For all have sinned, and come short of the glory of God* (Romans 3:23);

III. REPENTANCE LEADS TOWARD SOMETHING.

A person repents because he or she <u>believes</u>. Without belief, it is impossible to repent. And with <u>belief</u> also comes further obedience to the Word of God. This fact is expressed in Mark 16:16, which states: *He that believeth and is baptized shall be saved; but he that believeth not shall be dammed.*

In Acts 3:19, we are advised to "*repent and be converted.*" In Acts 2:38, we are commanded to "*repent and be baptized in the Name of Jesus Christ for the remission of sins.*" Repentance always leads toward something. True repentance is progressive, leading to better things.

Paul's message was always "repent and turn to God," as in the passage taken from Acts26:20: *But shewed first unto them of Damascus, and at Jerusalem and throughout all the coasts of Judaea, and {then} to the Gentiles, that they should repent and turn to God, and do works meet for repentance.*

IV. REPENTANCE IS THE FIRST STEP TOWARD REMISSION OF SIN.

Repentance is only the <u>first</u> step in the <u>remission</u> of sins. The words of Jesus in Luke 24:47 links repentance to remission of sins, two different things. Repentance - done by the sinner. Remission - done by God. *And that repentance and remission of sins should be preached in his name among all nations, beginning at Jerusalem* (Luke 24:47).

Though repentance alone is not salvation complete, it definitely is a required ingredient for salvation. Jesus proclaimed in Luke 24:47 that repentance would be linked to true Bible salvation and that this experience would <u>begin</u> at Jerusalem. New Testament salvation began at Jerusalem with the birth of the Church on the Day of Pentecost, and repentance was the first requirement for entrance into that Church.

As repeated over and over in this lesson. there is more to salvation than mere repentance. Peter explained much more about it in Acts 2:38: *Then Peter said unto them, Repent <u>and</u> be baptized <u>every one of you</u> in the name of <u>Jesus Christ</u> for the <u>remission of sins</u>, and ye shall receive the gift of the Holy Ghost.*

There are many other scriptures to verify that repentance is not the only necessary thing in the process of a saving experience, but it is the first <u>and</u> continued requirement.

IV. REPENTANCE IS A CONTINUAL PROCESS.

In the Book of Revelation, chapters 1 and 2, five of the seven churches of Asia were advised to repent. 1. Ephesus - Repent and do your first works. 2. Pergamos - Repent, I'll come suddenly. 3. Thyatira - Repented not. 4. Sardis - Repent. 5. Laodicea - Be zealous and repent:

Surely, anyone could learn the importance of repentance from these five scriptures.

Repentance is an ongoing process in serving God. Paul said, "*But I keep under my body, and bring it unto subjection, lest that by any means, when I have preached to others, I myself should be a castaway*" (I Cor. 9:27). Again in Romans 12:1, Paul proclaimed: "*I beseech ye therefore, brethren, by the mercies of God, that ye present your bodies a living sacrifice, holy, acceptable unto God, which is your reasonable service.* If you haven't repented, do it now!

LESSON V: IS WATER BAPTISM NECESSARY?

Lesson Focus: Water baptism, a very important doctrine, is ignored more by the modern church world than any other Bible truth. It is of prime importance that we recognize that baptism is not a choice, but a command! Water baptism by immersion in the Name of Jesus Christ is an absolute must to attain salvation. Most people of the church world today don't even believe that water baptism is essential, so they don't care how baptisms are performed, if ever. It is necessary first that they believe that they must be baptized, and then it will be possible to learn how.

> **Scripture Selection**: Mark 16:16: Mark 16:16
> *He that believeth and is baptized shall be saved; but he that believeth not shall be damned.*

I. IS WATER BAPTISM NECESSARY TO BE SAVED?

This lesson is started with the very important question: That this question should ever have to be asked is puzzling. Our Lord personally commanded baptism in two places: Matthew 28:19; Mark 16:16. Why would He have commanded it if it were not necessary? And if the commands of God are not pertinent, then what is?

Man has a rule of thumb; God has a rule of thumb. Here's God's rule:

II. NOTHING CAN BE ESTABLISHED AS TRUTH WITH ONLY ONE WITNESS.

But if he will not hear thee, then take with thee one or two more, that in the mouth of <u>two or three witnesses </u>every word may be established.(Matthew 18:16)

This is the third time I am coming to you. In the mouth of <u>two or three</u> witnesses shall every word be established. (2 Cor. 13:1)

Knowing this first, that no prophecy of the scripture is of any private (just one) *interpretation.* (2 Peter 1:20)

As you will notice, three separate scriptures are listed to verify the statement that more than one witness is needed to establish a doctrine. It isn't God that needs to have something stated more than once, it is man that needs it. No one in his right mind would entrust a supercomputer controlling all the operations of an entire corporation to anyone with just a one-time instruction on how to use it. No, no, no! It would take a lot of training. And so it is with doctrine. The Word of God states doctrinal truths in more than one place.

In this lesson you'll read far more than one Scripture affirming the necessity of water baptism for the remission (removal) of sins.

III. WATER BAPTISM IS A <u>COMMAND</u>, NOT A REQUEST!

There is a vast difference between a <u>command</u> and a <u>request</u>. Never does the Bible say, "If you feel like it," or "You ought to be baptized, but it's not necessary for salvation." Why would our Lord command baptism if it weren't necessary? The Scriptures very clearly declare that salvation and sin cannot share the same temple (our bodies); sins must be washed away in water by the Word of God - *That he might sanctify and cleanse it with the <u>washing of water </u>by* (using) *the word* (Ephesians 5:26)

In Matthew 28:19, Jesus <u>commanded</u>: *Go ye therefore, and teach all nations, **baptizing** them in the name of the Father, and of the Son, and of the Holy Ghost.*

In Mark 16:16, He stated: *He that believeth and is **baptized** shall be saved, but he that believeth not shall be damned.*

In Luke 24:47, again Jesus declared: *And that repentance and **remission** of sins should be preached in his name among all nations, **beginning** at Jerusalem.*

In St. John 3:5, *Jesus answered, Verily, verily, I say unto thee, Except a man be born of **water** and of the Spirit, he cannot enter into the kingdom of God.*

Titus 3:5: *Not by works of righteousness which we have done, but according to his mercy he saved us, by the **washing** of regeneration, and renewing of the Holy Ghost.*

I Peter 3:21: *The like figure whereunto even **<u>baptism</u>** doth also **now <u>save</u> us** (not the putting away of the filth of the flesh, but the answer of a good conscience toward God) by the **resurrection of Jesus Christ.***

Compare **baptism** and **resurrection** in the above Scripture from I Peter 3:21 to Romans 6:4: *Therefore we are buried with him by **baptism** unto death: that like as Christ was **raised** up from the dead by the glory of the Father, even so we also should walk in newness of life.*

If there is **no burial** (baptism), there can be **no resurrection!**

IV. WATER BAPTISM WAS ALSO COMMANDED BY THE APOSTLES.

In Acts 2:38 we read Peter's understanding of Jesus' last words on earth, and they concerned water baptism. *Then Peter said unto them, Repent, and be **baptized** every one of you in the name of Jesus Christ for the remission of sins, and ye shall receive the gift of the Holy Ghost.*

Peter was very convinced of the need for water baptism, because we read of him again in Acts 10:47,48 where he said: *Can any man **forbid water** that these should not be **baptized**, which have received the Holy Ghost as well as we?*

*And he **commanded** them to **be baptized** in the name of the Lord. Then prayed they him to tarry certain days.*

WATER BAPTISM is so important that the Holy Ghost commanded **Philip** to leave a mighty revival in Samaria to go down into the desert of Gaza to intercept an Ethiopian eunuch who needed baptism. After the eunuch invited Philip up into his chariot and asked him to explain the Scripture passage he was reading, *..Then Philip opened his mouth, and began at the same scripture, and preached unto him Jesus. [36]And as they went on their way they came unto a certain water; and the eunuch said, See, here is **water**, what doth hinder me to be **baptized**?* (Acts 8:35,36)   The answer to the eunuch's question is found in the next verse: [Acts 8:37]*And Philip said, If thou believest with all thine heart, thou mayest. And he answered and said, I believe that Jesus Christ is the Son of God.*

Philip **did** **not** tell the eunuch that baptism was **not necessary**. Instead, he informed him that he first must **believe.** Baptism devoid of belief is worthless. But because the eunuch believed, we read the following:

*And he commanded the chariot to stand still: and they went down **both** into the **water**, both **Philip and the eunuch**; and he **baptized** him.* (Acts 8:38)

In repudiation to the contention by some that water baptism is merely an outward sign of an inner cleansing, this baptism was **not** a public affair. It was performed in a desert oasis! If baptism were meant merely for a witness, why was it done where there was no audience?

Annanias, a devout Christian, was in the city of Damascus at the very time that the vicious Saul of Tarsus was headed to that city to arrest and destroy all the Christians there. The only biblical account of Annanias is in the baptism of Saul (Paul).   Paul, who became the greatest apostle in the New Testament, needed to be baptized in water. God told Annanias to go to the street named Straight for the specific purpose of baptizing Saul (Hebrew for Paul). This is the only biblical account of Annanias, but his baptism of Paul put him in the Bible. After Annanias laid hands on Paul and prayed for him, we read these words: *And immediately there fell from his eyes as it had been scales and he received sight forthwith, and arose, and **was baptized*** (Acts 9:18).

A converted Paul preached water baptism throughout his ministry. Let's read of this same Paul, who years later went to Ephesus and found **disciples**. He asked them a strange question, since they were already **disciples.** When he learned that they had not received the Holy Ghost as yet, his question was: *Unto what then were ye **baptized**? [5]When they heard this, they were **baptized** in the name of the Lord*

Jesus (Acts 19:1,5). Oh, yes, water baptism does make a difference!

IV. WATER BAPTISM REMITS (SENDS AWAY) SIN.

Acts 2:38 clearly states that baptism is specifically for the remission, or sending away, of sin. *Then Peter said unto them, Repent, and be baptized every one of you in the name of Jesus Christ for the* <u>**remission**</u> *of sin.*

In Acts 22:16, the apostle Paul retells his conversion and Annanias' instruction to him that he had received from God. Annanias said: *And now why tarriest thou? arise, and be baptized, and* **wash away thy sins,** <u>*calling on the name of the Lord.*</u>

I Peter 3:21 is even more specific about the purpose of baptism. Peter said, *The like figure whereunto even* **baptism** *doth also* **now save** *us by the resurrection of Jesus Christ (not the putting away of the filth of the flesh, but the answer of a good conscience toward God,)*

Every serious-minded person needs to take some time and carefully consider: *the* **washing** *of* **water** *by the word* in Ephesians 5:26: . The nominal church world is all too ready and willing to teach that this **washing** is done by the Word, or the Bible. That would be well and good if that were what the Scripture affirmed, but that is **not** the case! Notice particularly the wording, "*washing of* **water**." And, of course, if the Word (St. John 1:14; I John 1:1,2 - Jesus) does not **accompany** the **washing by water**, then only the body will be affected and never the soul.

V. HOW CAN ANYONE HONESTLY TEACH THAT BAPTISM IS <u>NOT</u> NECESSARY?

They can't. The answer is as simple as that. There is no Scripture text <u>anywhere</u> in the Word of God that states that water baptism is **not** necessary. The opposite is the case. There are multiple passages that **demand** water baptism. (We've listed several in this lesson already.)

So, what about the thief on the cross? What about him? The Church and New Testament salvation didn't begin until the Day of Pentecost, so the thief could not have been included in the New Testament plan of salvation. Second, the thief **may have been baptized** before he turned to crime. He could have been one of the multitude that forsook Jesus when the Lord preached that His disciples must drink His blood and eat His flesh. The Scripture plainly states that many were offended when He made those statements. So, it's just as fair to say he was baptized before he was crucified as it is to say he wasn't. Who knows? At any rate, it certainly isn't scriptural to definitely say that he was not baptized. Luke 24:47 informs us that the New Covenant had not yet taken place when the thief was crucified. Old Testament Laws did not demand baptism. The thief was still under the Law of Moses when he died, so he wouldn't have needed baptism to be saved.

What about our dead relatives?   They're gone, and there's not a thing that you or I can do to change that. There's a lot of things that we don't understand, but everyone **can** understand Scripture.

Walk with Me Through the Word

If you will let **Scripture**, and only **Scripture** talk, you won't have trouble with baptism.

We've given multiple Scriptures in this lesson to prove the necessity of water baptism - those who teach otherwise can produce **not one Scripture** that states that it is unnecessary!

Considering the affirmation of water baptism by so many great Bible witnesses, is it wise to deny it? Baptism is **not** a choice we can make. It is a **command** given by our Lord and affirmed by His disciples and Apostles. Now listen to what Paul had to say as a final word on the subject.

*But though we, or an angel from heaven preach any other gospel unto you than that which we have preached unto you, let him be **accursed*** (Galatians 1:8)*.*

Oh yes, it pays to be sure!

LESSON VI: THE CORRECT BIBLE BAPTISM

Lesson Focus: Everyone must understand that Matthew 28:19 is a **command**. To discover how to **perform** that **command**, a person must go to the Book of Acts where the only accounts of **actual** water baptisms are described. To follow the example of those that **heard** and **obeyed** the original **command** should be a safe practice to follow, even two thousand years later.

Scripture Selection: Matthew 28:19; Mark 16:16; Luke 24:47; Acts 2:38; Colossians 3:17.

*Matthew 28:19 Go ye therefore, and teach all nations, baptizing them in the **name** of the Father, and of the Son, and of the Holy Ghost.*

Mark 16:16 He that believeth and is baptized shall be saved; but he that believeth not shall be damned.

*Luke 24:47 And that repentance and remission of sins should be preached in his name among all nations, **beginning** at Jerusalem.*

Acts 2:38 Then Peter said unto them, Repent, and be baptized every one of you in the name of Jesus Christ for the remission of sins, and ye shall receive the gift of the Holy Ghost.

Colossians 3:17 And whatsoever ye do in word or deed, do all in the name of the Lord Jesus, giving thanks to God and the Father by him.

I. THERE ARE THREE RENDITIONS OF THE SO-CALLED GREAT COMMISSION.

The first written record in our Bible of Jesus talking about water baptism transpired shortly before His ascension, when He told His disciples, *Go ye therefore, and teach all nations, baptizing them in the **name** of the Father, and of the Son, and of the Holy Ghost* (Matthew 28:19). Though first in the four Gospels, this Scripture is **not** the **last one** made by the Lord Jesus. Matt.28:19 tells a person **what** to do in the salvation process.

The so-called Great Commission is mentioned in **three** places in the Gospels rather than just one, and in more explanatory language in the other two: Mark 16:16; Luke 24:47. The hyphenated word "so-called" is used to question whether there are not other Scriptures that deserve the title "Great Commission" more than does Matthew 28:19 . The Matthew utterance was made **prior** to the other two and confirmed by the fact that Jesus ascended immediately after voicing the accounts in Mark 16:16 and Luke:24:7. That is not to say that Matthew's account is not credible, but it can be said that it needs **more** Scripture to explain what the Lord was saying in that passage of Scripture.

II. WE NEED TO IDENTIFY THE PURPOSE OF EACH "GREAT COMMISSION."

Matthew 28:19 tells us **what** to do; Mark 16:16 tells **why** we should do it; Luke 24:47 tells **what happens** and that Jerusalem was where the message of **remission of sins** would **begin**.

29

The **what to do** is easily seen in Matthew 28:19: *Go ye therefore, and teach all nations, baptizing them in the name of the Father, and of the Son, and of the Holy Ghost:*

The **why we should do it** is seen in Mark 16:16: *He that believeth **and is baptized** <u>shall be saved</u>; but he that believeth not shall be damned.*

What happens and **where** is disclosed in Luke 24:47: *And that repentance and **remission of sin** should be preached in **his name** among all nations, **beginning** at Jerusalem.* Understand that the preaching the name of Jesus for the remission of sins didn't start until the Day of Pentecost in chapter two of the Book of Acts.

III. THE APOSTLE PETER WAS CHOSEN TO BE THE FIRST FOR THE CHURCH.

Peter was the first to preach the message of remission of sins in Acts 2:38: *Then Peter said unto them, Repent, and be baptized every one of you in the name of Jesus Christ for the remission of sins, and ye shall receive the gift of the Holy Ghost.* Notice also that Jesus used Peter to preach the message of remission of sins, thus fulfilling Matthew 16:18: *And I say also unto thee, That thou art Peter, and upon this rock I will build my church; and the gates of hell shall not prevail against it.*

Jesus told Peter in Matthew 16:18 that He would use him to lay the **foundation** for the Church, and in Acts 2:38: *...Peter said unto them, Repent, and be baptized every one of you in the name of Jesus Christ for the remission of sins, and ye shall receive the gift of the Holy Ghost.* With Peter's utterance of these words, the Lord fulfilled His word. In I Corinthians 3:11, the apostle Paul said: *For other foundation can no man lay than that is laid, which is Jesus Christ.* It appears that an overwhelming majority of the church world has chosen to build on another foundation.

IV. MATTHEW 28:19 MUST BE CONFIRMED WITH MORE SCRIPTURE

In Matthew 18:16, our Lord Jesus Christ stated the necessity of more than one witness. (More than one Scripture when Scripture is stated. More than one human witness when humans are involved). Matthew 28:19 is the **only** place in Scripture where that command was used. The verse needs more Scripture to explain its meaning. Matthew 28:19 stands alone. Had our Lord intended His words to be <u>repeated,</u> He most certainly would have said them again in another place to fulfill His own statement for the need of more than one witness.

Many advocates of baptism in the name of Jesus Christ go to the extreme by saying that Matthew 28:19 was not in the original copies of Scripture. If that is the only defense for baptism in the name of Jesus Christ, the case is lost. **No <u>original copies of Scripture exist anywhere</u>**, so how could anyone know whether the verse was there? There absolutely has to be more proof than that

V. MATTHEW 28:19 IS ABSOLUTELY CORRECT AS STATED.

It's the interpretation of the verse by the greatest percentage of the church world <u>that is wrong</u>!

If our Lord had intended that the exact words of this Scripture be used, then every apostle and Bible writer would have confirmed that. But they didn't. And they didn't repeat the Lord's exact words, but they **obeyed what He told them to do** by baptizing in the name of Jesus Christ. **Every baptismal record from Acts, chapter two onward, confirms that "Jesus Christ" is the name the Lord intended to be used in baptism and obey Matthew 28:19.**

Matthew 28:19 is not an error. The very opposite is true. Error is committed, though, when people **repeat** the words used by Jesus instead of <u>understanding</u> <u>what</u> <u>He</u> <u>meant</u> and **applying** the **Name**. Jesus did not say, "*Go and repeat me,*" but, "*...baptizing them in the **Name**...*" and this is precisely what occurred in the Book of Acts, chapters 2,8,10, and 19. Peter, Philip, and Paul all baptized in the Name of the Lord Jesus Christ. After all, Jesus said "name" rather than "names" in His commandment in Matthew 28:19 - "*...baptizing them in the <u>name</u> ...*" Our Lord said what He meant, and meant what He said. He instructed that we baptize in the <u>Name</u>. *8Then Peter, filled with the Holy Ghost, said unto them, Ye rulers of the people, and elders of Israel, 9 If we this day be examined of the good deed done to the impotent man, by what means he is made whole; ...12Neither is there salvation in any other: for there is none other **name** under heaven given among men, whereby we must **be saved**.* (Acts 4:8,9,12)

If in Matthew 28:19 the Lord had intended that we use other <u>names</u> (but He said <u>name</u> rather than name**s**), He would have given us a Name for the Father, because the Name of God certainly is not Father, and He would have given us a name for the Holy Ghost. He gave us only one <u>name</u>, His own, for there is no salvation in any other (Acts 4:12). Jesus intended that we <u>fulfill</u> His command, not <u>repeat</u> His words.

VI. GOD IS NOT THE AUTHOR OF CONFUSION, BUT...

Much confusion in church circles can be attributed to the fact that a single Scripture often is used to form a doctrine. This practice is <u>always</u> dangerous. God has mandated a formula by which all doctrine must be affirmed. This subject was addressed in Lesson 5, but repetition is helpful, often very necessary, when things of great value are considered. There is no subject greater than the eternal salvation of a soul.

God demands that **every word** be confirmed by **more** than one witness. No Scripture can stand alone. Scripture confirms Scripture. God does **not** fear that His Word be checked - He **demands** that it be done! God Almighty doesn't need to repeat Himself. **We** are the ones who may, and usually don't understand. For this reason, He demands that a Scripture be confirmed by at least **two** others. The reason for this is simple. We know what we **read**, but do we **understand**? The more Scripture to support a subject, the greater our comprehension of it.

We can't base a whole doctrine on one Scripture any more than we ordinarily can complete a simple sentence in one word. **We** need that the Lord repeat commands and instructions for our sake. We know what we read, **but** we don't always **understand** what He is telling us.

VII. DOES THE BOOK OF ACTS CONTRADICT MATT. 28:19?

If this were the case, we could believe none of the Bible! Acts 2:38, 8:16, 10:48, and 19:5 are all accounts of water baptisms in the Name of Jesus Christ in obedience to Matthew 28:19.

*<u>Acts 2:38</u> Then Peter said unto them, Repent, and be baptized every one of you in the **name** of Jesus Christ for the remission of sins, and ye shall receive the gift of the Holy Ghost.*
*<u>Acts 8:16</u> (For as yet he was fallen upon none of them: only they were baptized in the **name** of the Lord Jesus.) Acts 10:48 And he commanded them to be baptized in the **name** of the Lord.*
*<u>Acts 10:48</u> And he commanded them to be baptized in the **name** of the Lord. Then prayed they him to tarry certain days.*

Every baptism in the Book of Acts was done using the <u>Name</u> of Jesus Christ, and **every one** of them obeyed the instructions given by Jesus in Matthew 28:19. Baptizing in the Name of Jesus Christ is the <u>only</u> way Matthew 28:19 can be obeyed!

VIII. JESUS IS A NAME THAT IS VERY SPECIAL.

Our Lord <u>inherited</u> His name <u>from His Father</u> - *Being made so much better than the angels, as he hath <u>by inheritance</u> obtained a more excellent <u>name</u> than they (Hebrews 1:4).* Our Lord could not have inherited anything from His Father that His Father did not already <u>possess</u>. Jesus got His Name from His Father! Wow! That Name is so great and so marvelous that the whole family of God in heaven and earth carries it - *For this cause I bow my knees unto the Father of our Lord Jesus Christ, ¹⁵**Of whom** the **whole family** in heaven and earth is **named** (Ephesians 3:14,15).* The whole family of God has one name.

It's fairly easy to discover a family name. In normal circumstances we can learn the name of a family by a very simple procedure. All we have to do is get acquainted with one of the kids, ask him his name, and then we've learned the family surname. If the little guy's name is James Brown and he has the same name as his father, then his father's name is Brown. It's that simple.

If you asked the nominal Christian what the name of God is, he would probably answer, "God!" If you asked the name of the Holy Ghost, you would probably draw a, "I don't know." But if you asked, "What is the name of the Son?" you would get an immediate answer, "Jesus!" Well, now you've just discovered the <u>Family Name</u>, because the whole Family in heaven and earth bear the <u>same</u> name.

Mary and Joseph did not pick a name for her expected child. In fact, they didn't even <u>name</u> Him. He already had a name before He was born! He had His Father's Name! The angel did not tell Mary to **name** her son Jesus when he should be born. He said, *...thou shalt <u>**call**</u> his name JESUS...* Jesus was not named at Bethlehem, but <u>called</u> by the Name He was born with. Here's two Scripture verses to confirm that statement.

*<u>Matthew 1:21</u> And she shall bring forth a son, and thou shalt **call** his name JESUS: for he shall save his people*

from their sins.

Luke 1:31 And, behold, thou shalt conceive in thy womb, and bring forth a son, and shalt **call** his name JESUS.

IX. JESUS IS A NAME AGGRANDIZED MORE THAN ALL OTHER NAMES.

Jesus is a name far above <u>anything</u> in this <u>world</u> but <u>also</u> in that which is <u>to come</u>! Here are several scripture verses and their locations in your Bible.

Ephesians 1:20,21 Which he wrought in Christ, when he raised him from the dead, and set him at his own right hand in the heavenly places,

²¹ Far **above all** principality, and power, and might, and dominion, and every **name** that is named, <u>not only in this world, but also in that which is to come</u>.

Philippians 2:9 Wherefore God also hath highly exalted him, and given him a name which is **<u>above</u>** every **name**.

If God possesses any <u>other</u> name than the name of Jesus, it causes one of the greatest contradictions possible. Both Ephesians 1:20,21 and Philippians 2:9 assert that the name of Jesus is **above** every name. Ephesians 1:21 proclaims that this name is **above** all power, not only in this world, but in the future one as well. Where does that put any other name? Really, there is no conflict. Carefully consider the next point in this lesson.

X. JESUS IS THE NAME OF THE FATHER.

Hebrews 1:4 tells us that Jesus inherited His name <u>from</u> the Father, and since His name is Jesus, and He couldn't have inherited something that His Father did not possess, the Father must also possess the name JESUS. The whole family in heaven and earth share the same name (Eph. 3:15).

Jesus laid bold claim to the source of His name. He rebuked the hypocritical Jewish elite in John 5:43 by stating: *I am come in my <u>Father's name</u>, and ye receive me not: if another shall come in his <u>own</u> name, him ye will receive.* Jesus didn't come in His own Name, but in the Name of His Father. He carried the power of heaven on an earthly mission to redeem lost sinners.

XI. SALVATION DEPENDS ON EVERYTHING BEING DONE IN THE NAME OF JESUS.

And that includes water baptism. Colossians 3:17: *And whatsoever ye do in word or deed, do all in the name of the Lord Jesus, giving thanks to God and the Father by him* amens that statement. Water baptism entails both <u>word</u> - in the Name of Jesus Christ - and <u>action</u> - immersing the baptismal candidate in water. Bear in mind that Paul was not asking or suggesting that everything be done in word and deed, he was <u>instructing</u>. View this verse as a <u>command</u> and not a suggestion.

XII. HERE'S THE SUM OF THE MATTER.

Many people attempt to shrug off the necessity of being baptized in Jesus' Name with the statement, "Well, if Matthew 28:19 mean the same things as does Acts 2:38, why all the fuss?"

Well, as a first reason, the two are **not** the same thing. Matthew 28:19 is a **command**; Acts 2:38 shows how the **command** was carried out. Jesus did not want us to **repeat** His words; He intended that we **obey them**. When He commanded to baptize in the **Name** (not names), He meant precisely that. God has only **one** name.

It is a **Name** that will get you into or keep you out of heaven. I've identified that Name for you; so why don't **you** get baptized the same way that **every** New Testament convert was baptized, and that was in the Name of Jesus Christ?

Heaven and hell are realities, and **every** soul from the beginning to the end of time will spend eternity in one or the other. We pass through this life only once, and so decisions made here are eternal ones! God's Word makes it so clear that the **only** way that our sins can be **remitted** is through water baptism in the Name of Jesus Christ. The matter of salvation cannot be shrugged off. The **Name** is all-important, because there is no "...*salvation in any other; for there is none other **name** under heaven given among men, whereby we **must be saved***" Acts 4:12.

LESSON VII: YOU MUST BE BORN AGAIN

LESSON FOCUS: There is such a joyous feeling that accompanies repentance. A repentant sinner feels the burden of sin lifted from his soul. It's difficult for anyone to realize that there's yet more for them, and that they need that "more."

There are very few Bible promises preceded by the words, "Ye **must** be," but that is how the Lord introduced the New Birth experience. Repentance and baptism are **phases** of the New Birth experience just as there are phases in a natural birth. When a babe fully emerges from the birth canal, it will **always** cry and give distinct witness to the fact that a **new** baby has been **born!** And so it will be with the New Birth also. Being filled with God's Spirit (the Holy Ghost) completes the spiritual birth process.

Scripture Selection: St. John 3:1-9

1 There was a man of the Pharisees, named Nicodemus, a ruler of the Jews:

2 The same came to Jesus by night, and said unto him, Rabbi, we know that thou art a teacher come from God: for no man can do these miracles that thou doest, except God be with him.

3 Jesus answered and said unto him, Verily, verily, I say unto thee, Except a man be born again, he cannot see the kingdom of God.

4 Nicodemus saith unto him, How can a man be born when he is old? can he enter the second time into his mother's womb, and be born?

5 Jesus answered, Verily, verily, I say unto thee, Except a man be born of water and of the Spirit, he cannot enter into the kingdom of God.

6 That which is born of the flesh is flesh; and that which is born of the Spirit is spirit.

7 Marvel not that I said unto thee, Ye must be born again.

8 The wind bloweth where it listeth, and thou hearest the sound thereof, but canst not tell whence it cometh, and whither it goeth: so is every one that is born of the Spirit.

9 Nicodemus answered and said unto him, How can these things be?

I. NICODEMUS RECEIVED FAR MORE THAN HE CAME FOR, AND...

It seems that Jesus reverted to Old Testament terminology when He used such affirmative language as, "Ye **must**" when answering Nicodemus' unasked question. My opinion, of course, is speculative, but the Born-Again experience is not open to speculation. In order to enter the glories of God, one must be completely and totally changed, totally made over, hence the terminology, "born again." How can this transformation take place? How can one be redone, reborn, become completely new?

The salvation process is accomplished in several **phases** just as is the natural birth. Isaiah described it as *...precept must be upon precept, precept upon precept; line upon line, line upon line; here a little, and there a little:* (Isa. 28:10) And just as a premature natural birth usually causes complications or death, so does a premature extraction from the **saving process** cause calamity and often spiritual death altogether. The Lord chose a very unique man to introduce the truth of the New Birth.

Nicodemus, a ruler of the Jews, being a member of the Sandhedrin (Council of Seventy, the elite of Jewry), was purposely selected by the Lord Jesus to carry the New Birth truth to the **religious leaders** of the Jews. Nicodemus was an elder among the Jews, trained from childhood in their **religion**. He was a member of the Sandhedrin, the highest possible religious rank except for inherited positions, such as the High Priest and Levites.

Nicodemus came to Jesus under the cloak of night so that his fellow men would not see him. The truth he took home with him that night would never again allow him to comfortably dwell in his spiritual darkness. His completely changed view of spiritual things was dramatized when he and Joseph of Arimathaea begged the crucified body of Jesus from Pilate. The former nighttime visitor became a daylight witness to Pilate. He showed no fear of the man responsible for condemning his Lord to death on the cross. This type of fervency must assuredly have led him to the Upper Room on the Day of Pentecost and to a Born-Again experience.

II. EVERYONE MUST BE BORN AGAIN.

"To be brought into existence" is a good definition for "born." None of us existed before we were born. People cease to exist when they die, and that truth leads to the next statement: A **sinner** is **dead,** spiritually speaking. He does not exist in God's kingdom. He will be ignored by God on Judgment Day and banished from God's presence into the outer darkness of the real hell - the Lake of Fire. So, why must we be born again?

Romans 3:23 informs us *"For all have sinned, and come short of the glory of God;"* If **all** have sinned, and **all** have, then **all** are **sinners**. God's Word declares all sinners are **dead** in their trespasses and sins. **Dead** people do **not exist**. They have **ceased** to be. So they **must be** or would have to be born again if they were to live again on this earth. The born-again experience, however, is a spiritual rather than a fleshly experience.

A person's born-again experience will bring nothing but pride, and why not? In the first, natural birth of man, he is conceived of corruptible seed. He, like his father, will eventually die. In the New Birth, he is conceived of the **incorruptible** seed of the Holy Ghost, and just as Jesus Christ, born of and raised from the dead by the Holy Ghost to never die **again**, the Born-Again person in Him has the same promise of eternal life. It would be foolish **not** to want a Born-Again experience!

III. EVERY SEED BRINGS FORTH AFTER ITS OWN KIND. LET'S HEAR PETER NOW.
*Being born again, not of **corruptible seed**, but of incorruptible, by the word of God, which liveth and*

abideth for ever (I Peter 1:23).

From the first chapter of the Book of Genesis, verse 11, we learn the law of God concerning seeds. Every seed must produce of its own kind, reproduce the same kind of seed from which it was grown. Did you ever wonder how frustration can lead to anger to wrath to destructive action? The seed reproduces of its own, like itself, doesn't it? And so does love, joy, peace, longsuffering, gentleness, goodness, faith, meekness, temperance. (Galatians 5:22). All these bring peace, and Scripture calls our Lord "the God of peace."

In order to reproduce, every natural seed must give its life and then decay. This is true spiritually in order for anyone to receive the New Birth, the born-again experience. No two natures can exist in the same soul. And until the old nature in a person is mortified (killed), there can be no new birth.

Jesus Christ died in a <u>body</u> to provide a propitiation for sin, yet He lived in the Spirit. His natural death excused the believer forever from an eternal death. His rise from the grave guaranteed forgiveness to the repentant sinner and granted new life, a born-again experience, to "whosoever will." The life of the seed is in itself. In Him is life, and that life is **eternal**. The new life that a person receives in the New Birth has eternal value. This is <u>not</u> to say that a person cannot be lost after receiving the Holy Ghost. Since sin destroyed man <u>originally</u>, sin will <u>do the same again</u>, even **after** a New Birth experience. The born-again person, or the **reborn** person, receives power to overcome.

*Whosoever is born of God doth not commit sin; for his seed **remaineth** in him: and he cannot sin, because he is born of God* (I John 3:9).
For whatsoever is born of God overcometh the world: and this is the victory that overcometh the world, even our faith (I John 5:4).
We know that whosoever is born of God sinneth not; but he that is begotten of God keepeth himself, and that wicked one toucheth him not (I John 5:18).

Reborn individuals have power over sin when they let their seed (the Holy Ghost) work in them. The Holy Ghost refuses to succumb to the corruptible. And any time the Seed within us reproduces, it will duplicate itself, and that which is produced will glorify God.

IV. NOTICE HOW THE NEW BIRTH CHANGED PEOPLE IN THE NEW TESTAMENT.

<u>Peter</u>, the man who denied his Lord thrice <u>before</u> his conversion, also preached a mighty sermon on the Day of Pentecost **after** being filled with the Holy Ghost. His sermon brought **five thousand** people into the Church that day! And that is to say nothing of a later fact that Peter was so secure in the Holy Ghost that he **slept** between two guards on the night preceding his **execution!** What a difference the New Birth makes in a person!

Jesus surnamed <u>James</u> and <u>John</u>, the sons of Zebedee, "Sons of Thunder." Whether they were called the Sons of Thunder because they were loud, or whether their father was called Thunder, and their being his sons made them the sons of Thunder, is not known. Some things about them are known, however. They were self-seekers; they enlisted their mother to solicit Jesus to give each of them special positions in His kingdom. They were the ones who wanted to call fire from heaven upon their enemies. But notice what the Holy Ghost, New Birth experience did for each of them.

John wrote the Books of St. John, I, II, and III John, and the Book of Revelation. James willingly gave his life by beheading for the testimony of Jesus Christ. It's hard to think of a greater testimony than that of giving one's own life. Remember, these two brothers also forsook the Lord (Mark 14:50) the night of His arrest, but they lacked the power to overcome. This is why the Lord told all His disciples to stay in Jerusalem until they received the "promise of the Father." That "promise" came as the Holy Ghost in Acts, chapter two.

The New Testament is full of testimonies of Born-Again men and women. A person could spend **hours** in discoursing the dramatic difference in the lives of so many who walked with Jesus for 3 1\2 years, yet remained **unchanged** until **after** their New Birth experiences.

V. BEING BORN AGAIN IS JUST THAT - BEING BORN AGAIN!
Therefore if any man be in Christ, he is a new creature: old things are passed away; behold, all things are become new (II Corinthians 5:17).
For in Christ Jesus neither circumcision availeth any thing, nor uncircumcision, but a new creature (Galatians 6:15).

In the spiritual rebirth, the old person is replaced with a new one; the old desires succumb to new ones. Everything starts all over! A born-again person is spiritually brand new, and the experience feels so wonderful all over, praise the Lord!

VI. WOULDN'T YOU LIKE TO FEEL BRAND NEW?
If you haven't already experienced that life-changing experience in your life, you can. If you really wish for a chance to erase all the guilt of your past, you can. If you want a chance to start all over, you can. Every Christian at one time felt that way, and that's why they chose to grab onto the opportunity of being born again. And do you know what? You can also if you just want to. Here's how.

Repent, get baptized in the name of Jesus Christ, believe and receive the Holy Ghost. That's right from the Word of God.

Then Peter said unto them, Repent, and be baptized every one of you in the name of Jesus Christ for the remission of sins, and ye shall receive the gift of the Holy Ghost (Acts 2:38)

LESSON VIII: REST (THE HOLY GHOST BAPTISM)

Lesson Focus: In this lesson we want to show that the REST spoken of by Isaiah prophetically came to pass in the baptism of the Holy Ghost.

Scripture Selection: Isaiah 28:9-12; Joel 2:28,29

Isaiah 28:9 *Whom shall he teach knowledge? and whom shall he make to understand doctrine? them that are weaned from the milk, and drawn from the breasts.*

10 For precept must be upon precept, precept upon precept; line upon line, line upon line; here a little, and there a little:

11 For with stammering lips and another tongue will he speak to this people.

12To whom he said, This is the rest wherewith ye may cause the weary to rest; and this is the refreshing: yet they would not hear.

Joel 2:28 *And it shall come to pass afterward, that I will pour out my spirit upon all flesh; and your sons and your daughters shall prophesy, your old men shall dream dreams, your young men shall see visions:*

29 And also upon the servants and upon the handmaids in those days will I pour out my spirit.

I. HERE'S A QUESTION THAT NEEDS AN ANSWER:

Did God rest on the seventh day of creation because He was worn out, or was it for another reason? It certainly was not because He was tired, so it had to be for another reason. Everyone needs to understand that reason.

In our study of this subject, there are five questions that need an answer:
1. <u>What</u> is <u>Rest</u>?
2. To <u>whom</u> is it made <u>available</u>?
3. <u>When</u> did it become <u>available</u>?
4. <u>How</u> is it <u>recognized</u>?
5. **When** will it be <u>complete</u>?

II. WHAT IS REST? READ ON AND THIS LESSON WILL SHOW YOU.

*And on the seventh day God ended his work which he had made; and he **rested** on the seventh day from all his work which he had made (Genesis 2:2)*

For **every** New Testament **doctrinal** truth, there is an Old Testament type or shadow to foretell it. God laid the groundwork for the Holy Ghost baptism from the beginning of time. His resting on the seventh day of creation was <u>not</u> due to fatigue, but as an <u>example</u> or <u>type</u> for a New Testament event or experience. This is vividly displayed in Abraham of the Old Testament meeting a personage that provided a type (example) for the New Testament truth.

Melchizedek did not intercept Abraham on the latter's return from the slaughter of the kings because he needed Abraham's tithe from the spoils. The incident transpired for no other reason than to establish an order and provide a type for Jesus Christ, who, like Melchizedek, is both King and Priest. Seventh-day Sabbath-keepers stress the importance of a Saturday for a seventh-day Sabbath. This day is set aside by them for their day of rest. Most other denominations set aside Sunday, the first day of the week, as a day of rest. Under Grace in the New Testament, a seventh day observance becomes <u>unimportant</u>, but the purpose and reason for a Sabbath leads us into a greater truth.

Under the Law of Moses, Sabbath-keeping was instituted for a day of rest. <u>Rest</u>, not the number, became a type or example of a **Rest** that God would give to New Testament believers. "**Sabbath**" means **cessation**. The strict observance demanded by the Law to completely cease manual labor on the seventh day links the word **Sabbath** to seven. The two words become synonyms - they mean the same thing. You'll read quite a bit more on **seven** in this lesson.

God placed special emphasis on the word **rest** in the Book of Isaiah. He also provided an <u>identification</u> for a **rest** that would come "afterward," as Joel said in the second chapter of His Book. But God knew Israel to be hard hearted, so He used another example or type of something wonderful to come. He also used the many examples of cessation of work to drive home a great lesson.

Israel's banishment into Babylonian captivity for seventy years was precipitated by their refusal to observe a Sabbatical Year and allow their land to **rest** every seventh year. This was done for a period of four hundred and ninety (490) years. Israel thus <u>owed God </u>and their land <u>seventy</u> years of non-reaping, which was provided by their absence from their land while being in the captivity of Babylon and, later, Persia, for a total of seventy years.

The Word of God places great emphasis on **rest** throughout the Old Testament. And when an attempt is made to understand this emphasis, a tremendous truth is revealed. **Rest** in the Old Testament emerges as a <u>shadow</u> or <u>type</u> for the <u>Holy Ghost baptism </u>of the New Testament. Our lesson cites Old Testament incidents with corresponding Scripture to lay the groundwork for the Holy Ghost experience of the New Testament.

III. LOOK WHAT GOD PROMISED MOSES OF THE OLD TESTAMENT.
*And he said, My presence shall go with thee, and I will give thee **rest** (Exodus 33:14).*

Moses' greatest desire was to enter Canaan before he died, but because of his disobedience in striking the rock twice, God refused to let him. In Moses' mind, he felt he could finally sigh with relief after having led such a rebellious people as the Israelites to their destination.

Moses died at the age of 120 years. His death occurred mere weeks before Joshua led Israel across the Jordan River into the Promised Land. The Lord allowed Moses to pass on to his eternal rest before this event and spare him the ultimate disappointment of seeing others go where he could not. After bathing in the glory and splendor of heaven for just a few seconds surely convinced Moses that God keeps His word - Moses felt completely rested, something he couldn't do for the last forty years of his life on earth.

We all must be perfectly honest and admit that Moses' relationship with God far exceeded any of our own experiences. He enjoyed a complete infusion of the Spirit of God, so much so that when he descended from the mountain where he had spent forty days before God, his face shone so brightly as to require a veil. Apparently, Moses' **rest** while on earth was like that of Isaiah and Joel in knowing that a tremendously great experience with God would occur in the future - **rest** - the baptism of the Holy Ghost. It is the Spirit of God (called the Holy Ghost in the New Testament) that gives a person true **rest**. Several scriptures qualifying that statement appear later in this lesson.

Jesus promised that when the Spirit of Truth should come that the Spirit of Truth would teach His disciples all things. Moses spoke the Law as God revealed it to him. The difference in Moses' experience and that which we enjoy today is in the effect of the experience. Moses was full of the Holy Ghost, but he was not baptized in the Holy Ghost. It seems we're abusing semantics, but please be patient.

The Lord promised His disciples that they would be **baptized** with the Holy Ghost. When the Holy Ghost came, Scripture states that they were **filled** (Acts 2:4). There is no contradiction. When they were **filled**, they were filled so full that they literally ran over with the Holy Ghost. Not only were they filled, but they were also immersed, baptized in the Holy Ghost as the Spirit overflowed them. Notice their fire and fervor to save sinners. Their filling of the Holy Ghost was not only complete, but it ran over.

IV. NUMBERS. IS GOD HUNG UP ON NUMBERS?

No, of course not, but the number **seven** had a special relationship to the word **rest** in the Old Testament. Notice God's emphasis on **rest** in the following Scriptures.

*And he said unto them, This {is that} which the Lord hath said, To-morrow {is} the **rest** of the holy sabbath unto the Lord: bake {that} which ye will bake {to-day}, and seethe that ye will seethe; and that which remaineth over lay up for you to be kept until the morning (Exodus 16:23). And thou shalt number seven sabbaths of years unto thee, seven times seven years; and the space of the seven sabbaths of years shall be unto thee forty and nine years (Leviticus 25:8).*

Every **seventh day** of the year was set aside so servants and animals could **rest**. Also, the 10th day of the **7th** month (the Day of Atonement) was set aside as a **Sabbath** of **rest** (Leviticus 16:31). Every **7th** year was set aside as a Sabbath of rest for the **land** (Exodus 23:10; Leviticus 25:4).

The Year of Jubilee (the 50th year) was celebrated at the culmination of **7 Sabbatical years** (Leviticus 25:8). On the 50th year, Hebrew slaves were freed, debts were canceled, and land ownership reverted to original owners. Can you imagine the relief, the **rest** for his soul, that a Hebrew slave in the possession of a Hebrew master felt, knowing that his bondage could be no more than seven years? And then there were the former landowners who had fallen on hard times and had to sell their land. The hope they held in knowing that the land would revert to family ownership in the year following seven groups of 7, or the 50ᵗʰ year must have provided **rest** for their troubled souls. What a tremendous emphasis put on rest!

V. SPIRITUAL REST WAS NOT PROVIDED UNTIL AFTER JESUS ROSE FROM DEATH.

If any Old Testament person could have obtained permanent spiritual **rest**, it surely would have been a "man after Mine own heart," King David. But the following Scripture is David's own words. *There {is} no soundness in my flesh because of thine anger; neither {is there any} rest in my bones because of my sin.*

Strong language was used concerning the Israelites that followed Moses out of Egypt but never believed God. Their rebellion provoked this statement. *Unto whom I sware in my wrath that they should not enter into my rest* (Psalm 95:11). The writer of the Book of Hebrews added this*: And to whom sware he that they should not enter into his rest, but to them that **believed** not?* (Hebrews 3:18) Doubt and rebellion by the men of Israel kept every man, except two, above the age of twenty to die one by one in the wilderness before they could go into Canaan, which was the rest that even the most wicked among them desired. Caleb and Joshua were the only two men above twenty that actually made it into Canaan - they believed!

Unbelief will still keep a person from obtaining **rest**. Notice the following:
For if Jesus (Joshua) *had given them rest, then would he not afterward have spoken of another day* (Hebrews 4:8). **Another day** - this is where you and I come into the picture. *There remaineth therefore a rest to the people of God* (Hebrews 4:9). *Let us labour therefore* (Hebrew's author addressed New Testament saints, so the **us** means **us** of this present hour) *to enter into that rest, lest any man fall after the same example of **unbelief*** (Hebrews 4:11).

Though much attention was given to **rest** in the Old Testament, it totally evaded Old Testament people. David complained of no **rest** in his bones (Psalms 38:3). All Israel was denied **rest** (Psalms 95:11; Hebrews 3:11). Unbelief kept them from obtaining **rest** (Hebrews 3:18).

Joshua could not provide **rest** for Israel in the land of Canaan , but Scripture in Hebrews 4:11 gives assurance of **rest** to New Testament saints. Stephen, the first Christian martyr, gives New Testament believers powerful hope. The following Scriptures are his own words.

Acts 7:48,49Howbeit the most High dwelleth not in temples made with hands; as saith the prophet,

*⁴⁹Heaven {is} my throne, and earth {is} my footstool: what house will ye build me? saith the Lord: or what is the place of my **rest**?*

In uttering these words, Stephen informed those who heard him that **rest** is associated with a dwelling place, but never one built by the hands of men (Acts 7:48,49). So, in order to exactly describe what is meant by **rest**, let's allow the prophet, Isaiah, to shed some light on the subject.

*And in that day there shall be a root of Jesse, which shall stand for an ensign of the people; to it shall the Gentiles seek: and his **rest** shall be glorious (Isaiah 11:10).*

Stay focused on the subject of **rest** as we continue reading from the Book of Isaiah.

*For with **stammering lips** and **another tongue** will he speak to this people.   ¹²To whom he said, This {is} the **rest** {wherewith} ye may cause the weary to rest; and this {is} the refreshing: yet they would not hear (Isaiah 28:11,12).*

Wouldn't it be wonderful if we could find a New Testament account of these other tongues and stammering lips? Well, great news, we can!
And there appeared unto them cloven tongues like as of fire, and it sat upon each of them.
And they were all filled with the Holy Ghost, and began to speak with other tongues, as the Spirit gave them utterance (Acts 2:3,4).

What meaneth this? That very question was mouthed over and over from many throats on the Day of Pentecost after the Holy Ghost baptized all those who waited on "the promise of the Father." They certainly were blessed for having obeyed so fully the commandment of their Lord just before He ascended to heaven. While those who had just received the Holy Ghost continued to speak with "other tongues" (actually foreign languages they had never learned), the phenomenon was published aloud to thousands in Jerusalem. A predominant question that rang forth from the crowd - **"What meaneth this?"** was answered by Peter. He explained that those who were speaking many different languages as they were being baptized with the Holy Ghost were not drunk, "*...as ye suppose, But this is that which was spoken by the prophet Joel;*

¹⁷And it shall come to pass in the last days, saith God, I will pour out of my Spirit upon all flesh: and your sons and your daughters shall prophesy, and your young men shall see visions, and your old men shall dream dreams:
¹⁸And on my servants and on my handmaidens I will pour out in those days of my Spirit; and they shall prophesy:(Acts 2:16-18)

In Joel 2:28,29 where God promised to pour out His Spirit, Joel did not mention tongues. Isaiah the prophet did, and Peter explained the experience. When the skeptical Jews heard and witnessed tongues on the Day of Pentecost, Peter explained that what they **saw** (people receiving the Holy Ghost) and **heard** (the same people speaking with other tongues, languages) was the fulfillment of Joel and Isaiah's prophecy.

Joel did **not** say that people receiving the Spirit of God would speak in another language, because he didn't know they would. Isaiah did not know that stammering lips and **another tongue** would accompany the baptism of the Holy Ghost. But Peter linked the individual utterances of these two prophets together with his assertion *"that what you see and what you hear"* was the fulfillment of both Joel and Isaiah's prophecies.

VI.   SO, TO WHOM IS REST (THE BAPTISM OF THE HOLY GHOST) PROMISED?

Our wonderful Lord Jesus Christ said, *"Come unto me, all ye that labour and are heavy laden, and I will give you **rest**."*(Matthew 11:28)

In Acts 2:39, the Apostle Peter said, *"For the **promise** is unto you and to your children, and to all that are afar off, {even} as many as the Lord our God shall call."*

Wow! Praise God! The promise of a Holy Ghost baptism is *to you* (those who heard him), *to **all** afar off* (in distant lands, and in distant times), and to *as many as the Lord should **call*** (Acts2:39). And since **no** man can come to Jesus except the Spirit **draw** him, then God wants everyone baptized in the Holy Ghost! Remember, that God wants **all** to come. *The Lord is not slack concerning his promise, as some men count slackness; but is longsuffering to us-ward, not willing that any should perish, but that all should come to repentance* (II Peter 3:9).

VII. JESUS' RESURRECTION MADE THE HOLY GHOST BAPTISM AVAILABLE.

The Holy Ghost baptism was not given until **after** Jesus was glorified. That statement is affirmed in the following Scriptures.

John 7:38,39 He that believeth on me, as the scripture hath said, out of his belly shall flow rivers of living water.
39(But this spake he of the Spirit, which they that believe on him should receive: for the Holy Ghost was not yet {given}; because that Jesus was not yet glorified) (St. John 7:38,39).

The first outpouring of the Holy Ghost **Rest** could not happen until after the **beginning**, which was to take place at **Jerusalem** (Luke 24:47). Jesus Christ Himself left the following words for us .

*And that repentance and remission of sins should be preached in his name among all nations, **beginning** at **Jerusalem*** (Luke 24:47).

The message of the Apostles is the **only** New Testament ministry that **began at Jerusalem**. Jesus Christ and John Baptist both **began** their ministries outside Jerusalem, so Luke 24:47 could not have been applicable to either of their ministries. Peter's message on the Day of Pentecost was the first **after** the

beginning as stated in Luke 24:47. Peter preached that those who spoke in **other tongues** were doing so **as** they received the Holy Ghost!

VII. REST, THE HOLY GHOST BAPTISM, CLEARLY IDENTIFIES ITSELF.

On the Day of Pentecost, they **all** spoke with tongues. Isaiah *28:11(For with stammering lips and another tongue will he speak to this people, **and** Acts 2:15-17 For these are not drunken, as ye suppose, seeing it is but the third hour of the day. But this is that which was spoken by the prophet Joel; And it shall come to pass in the last days, saith God, I will pour out of my Spirit upon all flesh: and your sons and your daughters shall prophesy, and your young men shall see visions, and your old men shall dream dreams* **confirm** the fact that tongues (other languages) identifies a Holy Ghost baptism. Clearly, both prophets spoke of the Holy Ghost outpouring on the Day of Pentecost in Jerusalem, ca. 28 A.D.

Acts 10:44 and 46 states that the Jews who accompanied Peter, a Jew, to the home of Cornelius, a Gentile, were astonished that the Gentiles **also** received the Holy Ghost, because they **heard them speak with tongues!**

When Paul baptized the disciples of John the Baptist in the name of Jesus Christ at Ephesus, they received the Holy Ghost **and** spoke with **tongues** (Acts 19:6).

God's Word demands two or more witnesses to confirm a truth. The Book of Acts provides **three** instances where people receiving the Holy Ghost **spoke with tongues.** Scripture **never** states that anyone received the Holy Ghost **without** speaking with tongues!

VIII. YOU MAY NOW ASK, "WHEN WILL THE HOLY GHOST BAPTISM END?"

Our Bibles give us the answer to that question in I Corinthians 13:10: *But when **that** which is perfect is come, then that which is in part shall be done away.* And now you may wonder what the **that** in this verse is referring to. Again, our Bibles give us the answer.

The Church of Christ and others make an issue of the word "that" in this verse. Their argument is that the "**that**" is not a personal pronoun and couldn't, therefore, refer to Jesus Christ. They argue that the "that" in this verse is the completion of the New Testament. This occurred, according to their argument, when the last apostle died. They don't have a single, solitary Scripture to affirm their contention. John clearly refuted that argument in the very first verse of his first epistle. He skillfully describes the **That** as being nothing else and none other than Jesus Christ. Carefully read the following verse and see the meaning of the word for yourself.

*That which was from the beginning, which we have **heard**, which we have **seen** with our eyes, which we have **looked upon**, and our **hands have handled**, of the Word of life* (I John 1:1);

Any searcher for truth will readily concede that the **That** in the above scripture is talking of none other than our Lord Jesus Christ! And since that is the case, then the **that** in I Corinthians 13:10 is **not** talking about the completion of God's Word but about Jesus Christ Himself! So, our Lord hasn't returned yet for His Church, so expect more people to yet receive **Rest**, the **Holy Ghost**.

Why would anyone deny himself **rest**? The Holy Ghost baptism is for everyone. Jesus said, "*Come unto me, all {ye} that labour and are heavy laden, and I will give you **rest.***"

If you haven't sought for the gift of the Holy Ghost because you fear tongues, discard your fear. You do not need to seek tongues. Simply ask God for the Holy Ghost, let Him fill you, and you won't have to worry about other tongues. Tongues automatically come with the baptism of the Holy Ghost. Don't let the devil fool you into seeking the sign when all you need to do is seek the experience! *For the promise is unto you, and to your children, and to all that are afar off, {even} as many as the Lord our God shall **call*** (Acts 2:39).

Peter also said, "*But this is **that** which was spoken of by the prophet Joel;* (Acts 2:16)
Oh, my friend, don't you want **this** so you can have **That**?

LESSON IX: RIGHTLY DIVIDING THE WORD

Lesson Focus: Every Bible reader needs to know **how** to study the New Testament. Without that knowledge, many might founder in trying to find the plan of salvation. In this lesson we will endeavor to show that the New Testament is divided into three main sections, and the importance or relevance of each section to the plan of salvation.

Scripture Selection: I Timothy 4:16; II Timothy 2:14-18
I Timothy 4:16 *Take heed unto thyself, and unto the doctrine; continue in them: for in doing this thou shalt both save thyself, and them that hear thee.*
II Timothy 2:14-18 *Of these things put them in remembrance, charging them before the Lord that they strive not about words to no profit, but to the subverting of the hearers.*
15 Study to shew thyself approved unto God, a workman that needeth not to be ashamed, rightly dividing the word of truth.
16 But shun profane and vain babblings: for they will increase unto more ungodliness.
17 And their word will eat as doth a canker: of whom is Hymenaeus and Philetus;
18 Who concerning the truth have erred, saying that the resurrection is past already; and overthrow the faith of some.

As you enter this lesson, imagine yourself to be a live-game hunter. You would expect to find animals and birds in the country and many people in a city, so it would be a waste of time to hunt in a city. By the same reasoning, it would be futile to build huge housing complexes in sparsely populated areas for lack of people to occupy them. The same reasoning holds true in the study of the Word of God.

If the Bible student is interested in the life and ministry of Jesus Christ, he wouldn't search completely through the New Testament to find that information. For general information on Christian daily living, one certainly would not search the Book of Acts. It's very important to know where to look for what. This will also prevent the Bible reader from confusing subjects. For instance: Jesus said that he that **hateth** not his family was not worthy of the Kingdom of God. John, the beloved, said that he that hateth his brother is in danger of hell's fire. And there's an answer for this seeming-contradiction.

In every instance we must ask: Who is speaking? To whom is it spoken? Is the spoken word just to those who heard or for all people of all time? And the only way that we can accurately determine the answers to these questions is to understand the sections of the New Testament. Keep an open mind as you study.

Someone once said that if you would look in the **last** place **first** when searching for something, you could save a lot of time. A very frustrating question is, "Where did you lose it?" Well, if we **knew** where we had lost something, it wouldn't be lost, would it? But isn't it **always** irritable to search for something and have no real idea as to where to look?

Many people become totally confused when they read the Bible. For those who start reading in the New Testament, many get through Matthew only to bog down in Mark, because they're reading much the same material a second time. Many who get to the Acts of the Apostles and history, read on excitedly. They then get confused when the language of Romans appears to be so harsh and scolding. You see; they don't realize what it is for which they are searching, so they sometimes fail to find it.

Much more gold probably remains hidden and not mined than has ever been discovered, but where is it? For a serious prospector, a first decision has to be made: Where would gold **not** be found? He would then decide where he **most** likely would discover it. And then he would concentrate all his efforts on that area in an attempt to become rich. So now we come to the real purpose of **this** lesson.

We are first going to discuss the areas of the New Testament where the **full plan of salvation** can **not** be found, and then concentrate all our efforts in searching in the **right** place. That makes sense, doesn't it? All right; let's give it a try.

- **THE NEW TESTAMENT IS NOT ONE CONTINUOUS DOCUMENT.**
 Actually, the New Testament contains three categories or sections. The first section (the Gospels) includes Matthew, Mark, Luke, and John. The second section is The Acts of the Apostles. We commonly refer to this book as simply "Acts." The third section (Romans through Revelation) is composed of letters (epistles) written to churches, to people who already were Christians. The Book of Revelation is included in this section since it, too, was a letter (epistle) sent to established churches.

 In order to arrive at our goal, we'll approach these sections in this order: The Gospels first, the Epistles second, and then the Book of Acts last.

I. **THE FOUR GOSPELS BRING US "GOOD NEWS."**
 And the "good news" was preserved for us by four different writers - Matthew, Mark, Luke, and John. None of these writers tried to tell all they witnessed of Jesus in their walk with Him. They couldn't have done it had they tried. In fact, John said that the world could not contain all the books it would take to tell all they had witnessed.

 Only two of the Gospel writers actually walked with Jesus. Luke and Mark wrote what they had learned from those who had actually walked with Him. In his opening statement of his first book, Luke stated that "many" had endeavored to set in order the things that Jesus had done. So, as you read the Gospels, know that they were confirmed by "many witnesses." Let's examine these rich Books and see exactly what they <u>did</u>, and then see what they <u>didn't do</u>.

The four Gospels describe: (1) the birth of Jesus Christ; (2) His ministry; (3) the calling of the disciples; (4) the giving of the Great Commission. Commonly thought to be recorded in the Book of Matthew only, the Great Commission was actually recorded in three of the four Gospels. We find this Commission recorded in Matthew 28:19; Mark 16:15,16; and Luke 24:47.

All that has been written concerning the Gospels, addressed things the Gospels did, but there were things that they <u>didn't do</u>. Let's look at the first one on this list:

(A) No church was founded in the Gospels. Our Lord Jesus told of a **<u>future</u>** building of His Church. The New Testament Church didn't come into being until the Day of Pentecost in an upper room at Jerusalem. Notice how the Lord said "will" in the following Scripture:

And I say also unto thee, That thou art Peter, and upon this rock I <u>will</u> build my church; and the gates of hell shall not prevail against it (Matthew 16:18). The Lord didn't say "...*upon this rock I <u>am</u> building,* " but "...*upon this rock I <u>will</u> build*." "Will" tells of a <u>future</u> building of the Church. Luke affirmed that the **beginning** of the New Testament Church was futuristic. *And that repentance and remission of sins should be preached in his name among all nations, beginning at Jerusalem* (Luke 24:47).

The building of the Church was a task relegated to the apostles, which was to happen **after** Jesus' ascension. See Matthew 16:18 (*I will build*); St. John 7:38,39 (...*spake he of the Spirit which they* **should** (or will) *receive...*); Luke 24:47 (...***beginning*** (starting at) *Jerusalem*).

(B) No one received the Holy Ghost in the Gospels, according to John's Gospel.

He that believeth on me, as the scripture hath said, out of his belly shall flow rivers of living water.
[39] *(But this spake he of the Spirit, which they that believe on him should receive: for* **the Holy Ghost was not yet given***;* <u>because</u> *that* <u>Jesus was</u> <u>not</u> <u>yet glorified</u>.*)* (John 7:38-39).

John enclosed his explanation of Jesus' words in parenthesis so that they would not be confused as being a part of the Lord's utterance. John appears to have been very conscientious about explaining that the Holy Ghost baptism did not take place until after the Lord ascended to heaven. That certainly would have been the Lord's glorification, and until that happened, the Holy Ghost baptism did not take place.

(C) No one was saved in the Gospels. And about now you may be thinking, "What about the thief on the cross?" The thief on the cross was justified before God the same way that any other Jew would who offered a sacrifice in the Temple would have. It is highly improbable that the thief would have bothered to offer a sacrifice during that year, considering his lifestyle. But in light of his dying on a cross without having offered one, and having no promise of peace after death, he called upon the Lamb of God, Who hang dying alongside him. Jesus became his **sacrifice** to satisfy the Law of Moses. The thief was justified because of his **Sacrifice**. He was a Jew, a descendent of Abraham. He, thus, will be judged according to the Law of Moses.

Under New Testament precepts, the thief couldn't have been saved. His sins would not have been remitted. **Jesus** Himself said that **repentance** and **remission** of **sins** would **begin** (start at) Jerusalem, and He said those words **forty days after his crucifixion** on the Mt. of Olives just prior to His ascension. If repentance and remission of sins was <u>not</u> possible at the time that Jesus stated these words just before His ascension, then repentance **with** <u>remission</u> (removal) of sins would not have been available to the thief on the cross. He was justified before God by Moses' Law. The New Covenant or New Testament didn't begin for nearly two months after the thief died. *And that repentance and remission of sins should be preached in his name among all nations, **<u>beginning</u>** at Jerusalem* (Luke 24:47).

The **beginning** of remission of sins **began** at Jerusalem, and the **only** account of a **beginning** of any ministry in the New Testament is found in the second chapter of Acts only, and more specifically, in Acts 2:38,39.

It's very apparent that the plan of salvation is not recorded or shown **anywhere** in the <u>Gospels</u>, so we must search elsewhere for this information. Let's explore the next largest group of Books in the New Testament - the Epistles - and look for this plan. By eliminating every **impossible**, we can settle on the only **possible**.

II. THE EPISTLES PROVIDE INSTRUCTIONS FOR CHRISTIAN LIVING.

The Epistles are letters written to saved people, to churches filled with saved people, and **never** was there an epistle written or addressed to sinners. The people to whom the Epistles were addressed did not **need** to read about the plan of salvation; they were Christians already. They didn't need to be told how to be saved; they had already experienced salvation!

The Epistles describe how God's New Testament people are to **live, act,** and **worship** - no more, no less. So, what is **missing** in the Epistles? **<u>First</u>**, there's not a single record of the founding of a church, so we can't determine **how** its members became Christians. In them, there is not a single instance of where the plan of salvation was presented to a lost person. **<u>Second</u>**, there's no record of anyone receiving the Holy Ghost in the Epistles. **<u>Third</u>**, there is **no** plan of salvation prescribed for the sinner, so the reader of these Books could remain lost unless he had already found the plan of salvation elsewhere in the Word of God.

The Epistles were **never** intended to be used as a blueprint for salvation. A lost person would search futilely for salvation in them. They were not written to show people how to be saved. Their sole purpose is to tell people how to live, act, and worship.

We've now gone through sections one and three of the New Testament, and still we haven't found the plan of salvation. There's only one section left. Let's look at this Book.

III. THE ACTS OF THE APOSTLES - JUST WHAT WE'VE BEEN SEARCHING FOR.

The Acts of the Apostles, commonly called "Acts" is the Book everyone should search **first** when searching for salvation. Acts contains actual accounts of churches being founded, people baptized in water after repentance in obedience to the Great Commission, and actual accounts of people being filled with the Holy Ghost, and what they did as they received the Holy Ghost.

Acts is the only section of the New Testament that tells and shows a person how to be saved. It is the **only** Book in the New Testament that explains St. John 3:5 (*...ye must be born again.*); Matthew 28:19 (*...baptizing them in the **Name**...*); Joel 2:28 (*...I will pour out of my Spirit...*), and Isaiah 28:11 (*...and another tongue...*). All these Scriptures relate to the Born-Again experience, and since Acts is the **only** Book in the **entire** Bible that **explains** and clarifies this experience, shouldn't a person study it **very, very,** carefully?

IV. SO, WHERE ONLY CAN THE PLAN OF SALVATION BE FOUND?

1. In the Gospels? No. No one's sins were remitted in the Gospels.
2. In the Epistles? No. The Epistles are letters written to <u>saved</u> people.

• **Where Then?**

The plan of salvation is found in the Book of Acts, and only in Acts.

Only the sincere will sincerely search. Even if a person cares nothing for his own soul, surely he should consider those that look to him for advice. We only pass this way once, and it's extremely important that we don't foul that one time through.

Jesus Christ advised the Jews to search the Scriptures. Paul urged Timothy to study to show himself approved unto God. <u>Second-hand</u> information will not stand as a <u>first-class excuse</u> in the presence of God. The really pitiful thing about misguided souls, though, is the fact that the Bible <u>is</u> understandable to those who will study to understand.

This lesson has not been presented to promote a denomination - every denomination should realize the three distinct sections of the New Testament. Every word of God is important, but it's essentially important to know to whom a particular Scripture was written or quoted, when, where, and why it was quoted. It is necessary to know and recognize the three sections of the New Testament.

Paul advised in II Timothy 2:15 to...*Study to shew thyself approved unto God, a workman that needeth not to be ashamed, rightly dividing the word of truth*. Need more be written about the importance of the three sections of the New Testament.

51

LESSON X: Gifts of the Spirit

Lesson Focus: Special emphasis should be placed on the fact that a gift of the Spirit enriches a person, but does not make him better. The gifts of the Spirit are given to born-again people, people already filled with the Spirit. The gifts are not evidences of salvation or witnesses that the receiver has reached a higher spiritual plateau, but merely proof that a generous God loves to give to a hungry soul. If it takes humility to receive a gift, then continued humility is necessary for the proper use of that gift.

Scripture Selection: Corinthians 12:1, 4-13:

1 Now concerning spiritual gifts, brethren, I would not have you ignorant.

4 Now there are diversities of gifts, but the same Spirit.

5 And there are differences of administrations, but the same Lord.

6 And there are diversities of operations, but it is the same God which worketh all in all.

7 But the manifestation of the Spirit is given to every man to profit withal.

8 For to one is given by the Spirit the word of wisdom; to another the word of knowledge by the same Spirit;

9 To another faith by the same Spirit; to another the gifts of healing by the same Spirit.

10 To another the working of miracles; to another prophecy; to another discerning of spirits; to another divers kinds of tongues, to another the interpretation of tongues:

11 But all these worketh that one and the selfsame Spirit, dividing to every man severally as he will.

12 For as the body is one, and hath many members, and all the members of that one body, being many, are one body: so also is Christ.

I. MUST A PERSON SPEAK IN TONGUES TO BE SAVED?

This question is generated by a Scripture found in I Corinthians 12:30. This is seemingly the favorite tool of those who resist tongues in the church. It is a pet argument in trying to prove that everyone doesn't speak in tongues when receiving the Holy Ghost. Before attempting to answer the question, the questioner needs to look at chapter one, verse two, of this same Book. Read along:

Unto the Church of God which is at Corinth, to them that are sanctified in Christ Jesus, called to be saints, with all that in every place call upon the name of Jesus Christ our Lord, both theirs and ours." (I Corinthians 1:2)

It is evident that this entire Epistle was written to a church, to people that already knew how to be saved and had already experienced salvation. The author, therefore, was not telling them how to get saved, but to explain Spiritual gifts given to believers. He explained the use of the gift of tongues extensively in chapter fourteen of this Book. He also explained that the purpose for the gifts being given is to enrich the receiver when he stated, *"is given to profit withal."*

Much emphasis today is placed on "spirituality." Mystic religions are growing by leaps and bounds as the spiritually-gullible fall victim. The 1960's witnessed a tremendous spiritual upheaval within many of the older denominations with the appearance of the "Jesus People," later to become synonymous with the Charismatic movement. In recent years, the Assemblies of God, Pentecostal Church of God, The Four-Square Gospel Church, and other trinity Pentecostal congregations have joined the Charismatic movement. Yet more recently, hundreds of Oneness Pentecostal churches have followed the lead of the others and have joined this movement.

Suddenly, it seems, there is tremendous restlessness within the Oneness movement, and instead of a hunger and thirst to return to fasting, all-night prayer, awe over the Word of God, and fervent evangelism that, in years gone by, converted thousands of nominal church members to Oneness Pentecostalism, many are being enticed with mysticism.

Embracing and manifesting a gift of the Spirit does not make the user extra spiritual or extra holy, but try to explain that to those who witness the operation of these gifts. A good rule of thumb to use when witnessing the operation of the gifts is to ask yourself the question, "Who seems to be receiving the glory?" And don't feel bad about making a judgment because, "...he that is spiritual judgeth all things..."(I Cor. 2:15) When the emphasis is placed on the gift or on its user rather than on the Giver, something is definitely wrong.

The purpose of this entire lesson is to de-emphasize the gift, any of the nine, and magnify God, the Giver of all gifts. Second, it shows that all Spiritual gifts are good - **all** of them , and not just the gift of tongues only. May we never put more or less importance on anything than the Lord intended. Now, let's consider the nine gifts given by our Lord:

1. Wisdom
2. Knowledge
3. Faith
4. Prophecy
5. Miracles
6. Gifts of healing
7. Discernment
8. Tongues
9. Interpretation

II. THE GIFTS OF THE SPIRIT CAN BE CATEGORIZED INTO THREE GROUPS.
For the sake of memory, read the listed gifts aloud, also.

The Gifts of Revelation are:
1. A Word of wisdom
2. A Word of knowledge
3. A Discerning of spirits

The gifts of revelation are so called because each of them imparts something to the believer that he can not learn or acquire any where but from God. The Spiritual gifts of wisdom, knowledge, and discernment of spirits endow extraordinary portions of these attributes to the receiver.

The Gifts of Power are:

1. Faith
2. The Working of miracles
3. Gifts of healing

The **faith** listed here is a special gift of faith upon which the other two power gifts hinge, for neither miracles nor healing could ever be done without extraordinary faith. Notice that the Word uses "gifts" rather than "gift" for healing to emphasize that no one holds the "gift" of healing, but "gifts" are available to many in need of healing. **Prophecy** entails not only preaching, but the actual forecasting of future events as God anoints. No one can argue that the working of miracles is beyond the power of man, and being so, miracles can be performed only by the power of God working within a person.

C. The Gifts of Utterance are:

1. The Gift of prophecy.
2. The Gift<u>s</u> of tongues - divers (different) kinds of tongues.
3. Interpretation of tongues.

Utterance gifts mesmerize people in about the same fashion as ventriloquism or magic sleight-of-hand tricks do. But unlike either of these, the utterance gifts are genuine. They can be performed only under the inspiration or anointing of God. Sadly, these gifts are <u>often</u> <u>faked</u>, and spiritually-shallow people fall prey to the deception. Pay particular attention to the next point.

III. FIRST CORINTHIANS WAS WRITTEN WITH A DEFINITE GOAL IN MIND.

I Corinthians, chapter 12, was written to combat polytheism (the worship of many gods). Paul understood that although the Corinthians Christians had been born again, that they also had been subjected to the pagan worship of multiple gods (polytheism). He explained that though there are 9 gifts altogether, that did not mean that there is a separate god for each gift, but that they all come from the same Spirit. He addressed former pagans in this Epistle, whose superstitions died hard. They were accustomed to revering a god for every occasion, such as a god for planting, one for harvest, etc.

Contrary to the philosophy of heathenism where all gods were to be feared, the God of the 9 Spiritual gifts gives to enrich the receiver, and thus enrich the entire church! Paul explained that each of these gifts works harmoniously with all the others in the same fashion that different members of the human body complement other members: limbs, nerves, etc. And just as each member of the human body is not a separate entity, neither does 9 separate Spiritual gifts make 9 Spirits or 9 gods!

And there are diversities of operations, but it is the same God which worketh all in all (I Corinthians 12:4).

When each of the nine gifts is used scripturally, the one true God of glory will be exalted in the hearts of those that behold. There are myriad reasons offered by those who resist the fact that the gifts of the Spirit are still operational in these end times. By far the most prevalent of all the attacks is the question asked next in this lesson.

IV. DO ALL SPEAK IN TONGUES?

To everyone who has already enjoyed the experience of communing with the Lord in God's own language, this question appears almost ridiculous. But in answer to the question, another question needs to be answered first. Is the body all eyes, all ears? That would present a grotesque being, to put it mildly. If the Church were only one thing, how ineffective, uninviting that church would be. No, everyone in the Church (church services) does not speak in or with tongues, but everyone who receives the Holy Ghost will speak with tongues while receiving, and it won't be because the person is compelled to do so. It is a joyous, precious moment. Few people throughout the history of the New Testament Church could claim possessing and exercising all nine gifts, so, no, they did not all possess the gift of tongues. A great percentage of modern Pentecostal adherents don't even manifest one Spiritual gift, let alone exercising all nine!

Much space has been given to the subject of tongues in this manual for definite reasons. Despite all the resistance against the subject, the use of tongues in private prayer and public worship is practiced in many denominations today. No longer is their use confined to or claimed by Pentecostal worshipers, only. Millions, worldwide, not only claim but extol the experience in glowing terms. Tongues, therefore, need explained, their proper use examined, and the difference between the gift tongues and other tongues.

Contrary to modern thinking, Paul did not **exalt** the gift of tongues, but he did defend its representation and necessity in the present-day church. He wrote: *Covet earnestly the best gifts.* Did he actually advise: *Covet the gifts best for the receiver and for the church*? Probably, since the entire chapter seems devoted to impressing upon his readers that each gift is given for edification. Some Christians might rather have the gift of wisdom, of knowledge, or the working of miracles than the gift of tongues. Any Holy Ghost-filled believer can receive one, two, or all of the gifts. It's entirely up to the believer. It depends entirely on how much he or she desires them.

Again, Paul didn't over-emphasize the use of tongues, but neither did he relegate the issue to one of no importance. For those who desire a Spiritual gift, they may covet any one or all of the nine. No one has to start or stop with the gift of tongues. God wants to impart every one of them to His people. "So, what," you might ask, "must I do in order to receive a gift of the Spirit?" Look at the very next statement for an answer to your question.

V. GOD GIVES SPIRITUAL GIFTS TO BELIEVERS.

The gifts are given so that individual believers might profit, or be strengthened, by them and edify the church by and through that strength. Never can anyone claim a higher spiritual plateau because he or she exercises one or more of the Spiritual gifts. God does not give Spiritual gifts to spiritual people! He gives them to Spirit-filled believers. No one can receive anything without believing. And when a person receives a Spiritual gift, that does not make him better; it simply makes him better <u>equipped</u> to do service for God! Donning a military uniform doesn't make anyone a soldier. It's how well the recruit represents the uniform that makes him one. The same reasoning holds true in spiritual matters, also. Receiving a Spiritual gift does not automatically produce a super spiritual achiever. Receiving a Spiritual gift does, however, <u>equip</u> a believer to do greater things for God. Beware, then, lest pride also cause the loss of that which has been received!

Without argument, the gift of tongues has been the most emphasized of all the nine gifts available to a believer. Why this over-emphasis on just this one gift? Hopefully, you can find that answer under the next heading. Speaking with tongues is important, but just how important?

VI. TONGUES ARE IMPORTANT BUT NOT NECESSARILY THE MOST IMPORTANT.

They are very valuable for the church, and anyone who would teach otherwise is refuting the Word of God. Tongues, however, are not the <u>only</u> gift of the Spirit. They should not be exalted above nor stressed less than any of the other eight gifts.

Tongues appeal to people because of their mysticism, which is not good since this places too much importance on the gift rather than on the Giver.

Tongues are easy to imitate, which, sadly, insincere people do rather often. Most of us know one language only, so we have to heavily rely on God to detect the sincere and the fakes. The exclamation, "Oh, I can detect a false message in tongues any day!" is rather pretentious unless you, of course, are a skilled linguist. Most people aren't even skilled in their own native language, let alone being expert in others. No, you can <u>not</u> spot a fake tongue every time, no matter what you say! Much has gone forth in tongues, supposedly, and has even been "interpreted," yet is nothing more than nonsense. We need to know them that work among us!

People literally flock to hear someone "minister in the spirit." Why doesn't someone parade the gift of a word of wisdom around the country? Supposed "faith-healers" have been in abundance over the years, and you can even learn how to speak in tongues, according to some people, but how about simulating a good miracle at least once a week? You see, the gift of tongues is only one out of nine available gifts. Desire the one, to be sure, but not slack in seeking for the other eight.

It's wonderful to communicate with the Lord in a language that is completely unknown, even to the devil. Satan hates the gift of tongues, because he can't understand what is being said, and that infuriates him. That is only one reason why he so hates the gifts of God. As you remain faithful, the Lord will endorse His gifts. You'll feel the genuine in your spirit.

The <u>gift</u> of tongues (a gift of the Spirit) must not be confused with <u>another tongue</u> or other tongues prophesied in Isaiah 28:11 and experienced first in Acts 2:4. Other tongues are evidence of the Holy

Ghost baptism. The difference between <u>other</u> <u>tongues</u> and the <u>gift of tongues</u> is addressed in detail in the next lesson.

VII. SO WHERE DOES ALL THIS PUT TONGUES IN IMPORTANCE?

Nothing that we could do or say would ever alter the importance for tongues in the Church. God made and used this gift many times in Scripture. Peter informed us that the gift of the Holy Ghost is to those "afar off (distant lands and distant places). When the Holy Ghost came the very first time, it came speaking other tongues or languages (Acts 2:4; 19:6). The <u>gift</u> of the <u>Holy Ghost</u> is **not** the same as the <u>gift of **tongues.**</u> More on that later.

To say that tongues are not important or necessary is to say that <u>none of the gifts are important</u>. Some churches actually believe and teach this! Paul, then, just wasted two whole chapters advising about something that is unnecessary! And that is not a very intelligent assumption either!

Each and every gift is given to profit the receiver, who will then edify (build up) the church. It is at these times that we see the person blessed with the gift, and the Church being blessed with the operation of the gift. The gift, then, becomes something that the receiver can profit with, or withal. *But the manifestation of the Spirit is given to every man to profit withal* (I Corinthians 12:4).

The Book of First Corinthians is one of two letters Paul wrote to the Church at Corinth (located in present-day Greece). Much has been said about tongues being the cause of divisions in that church. Such a statement is preposterous, considering that in chapter fourteen of this same Book, Paul said, "I would (wish) that you all speak in tongues" (Paraphrased). Common sense would tell us that if tongues be the cause for divisions in a church, then the absence of tongues should guarantee unity.

There undoubtedly are many reasons why people don't accept tongues, but simply because they're not understood shouldn't be cause for rejection of the gift. Because tongues are faked too many times is no true cause for rejection either. Be up front on the issue and ask whether the gift is being rejected or the one who presents it. Pure distaste for a person or his actions doesn't always mean that the thing being presented by that person is fake.

Again, tongues, and not a simulation of them, are <u>very</u> important to the Church - not the <u>most</u> important, necessarily, but very important, since....

VIII.   OUR GOD GAVE ALL OF THE GIFTS OF THE SPIRIT TO BE USED.

And may we never fall into the snare of shunning a particular gift because we do not understand it, or its operation makes us uncomfortable.

If you're uncomfortable during the operation of a gift, two questions need an answer. First: "Is what I'm witnessing genuine?" Second: "Am I genuine?" If you have a "yes" for both questions and still feel uncomfortable during the operation of a gift, you have a problem! Discomfort should never be experienced in a Holy Ghost-filled saint during the manifestation of any of the gifts of the Spirit.

Wisdom, the first mentioned of the nine gifts of the Spirit, genders peace in a soul, even when wisdom delivers a rebuke. Sounds odd, but it's true. Knowledge and Faith. What powerful gifts! Who would anyone not want either of them? And yet, both of these gifts are in the same group with the gift of tongues. Why want just one or two? Why not seek for all of them?

Let's stress one more very important point. In the operation of any gift of the Spirit, the receiver will be enriched, the church will be edified, and God will be glorified. So, now we ask:

IX. MUST A PERSON POSSESS A GIFT OF THE SPIRIT TO BE SAVED?

If you just identified with that question, you've missed the point. The nine gifts of the Spirit are just that - they're gifts. Don't cost anything; can't be earned; can't be bought - they're gifts. Everyone needs at least one Spiritual gift! They're free for the asking.

To too many believers, possessing the gift of tongues seems to be the ultimate of spiritually for them, but that is just not the case. Tongues are important, very important, but no more important than any one of the other eight gifts. One genuine miracle would convert thousands. Could we ever say the same for someone speaking in tongues?

This lesson should not be interpreted as being anti-tongues. The opposite is the case. Tongues were instituted for the New Testament Church, and they are still available and necessary in the church of today! No church should be comfortable without the gifts of the Spirit - all nine of them.

LESSON XI - AN OTHER TONGUE AND OTHER TONGUES

Lesson Focus: Whether it be a Spiritual tongue or **an other** tongue, we need to understand the operation of each. Many ministers remark of someone who spoke in a "heavenly language" when he or she received the Holy Ghost. This is completely erroneous, as this lesson will endeavor to prove.

Irrefutably, **an other** tongue or **other** tongues (same thing) are heaven-sent and Spirit-given, but this tongue (language) is not a heavenly language. The language that Holy Ghost recipients utter when filled with the Spirit is a foreign language spoken somewhere on earth.

This statement will be received with shock by many people, but, hopefully, this lesson will clear up this point.

Scripture Selection: Isaiah 28:10-12; Acts 2:4-8,16-17; 10:44-47
    Isaiah 28:10-12 For precept {must} be upon precept, precept upon precept; line upon line, line upon line; here a little, {and} there a little:
    11 For with stammering lips and another (an other) *tongue will he speak to this people.*
    12 To whom he said, This {is} the rest {wherewith} ye may cause the weary to rest; and this {is} the refreshing: yet they would not hear.
    Acts 2:4-8 And they were all filled with the Holy Ghost, and began to speak with other tongues, as the Spirit gave them utterance.
    5 And there were dwelling at Jerusalem Jews, devout men, out of every nation under heaven.
    6 Now when this was noised abroad, the multitude came together, and were confounded, because that every man heard them speak in his own language.
    7 And they were all amazed and marvelled, saying one to another, Behold, are not all these which speak Galilaeans?
    8 And how hear we every man in our own tongue, wherein we were born?
    Acts 2:16,17 But this is that which was spoken by the prophet Joel:
    17 And it shall come to pass in the last days, saith God, I will pour out my Spirit upon all flesh:
    Acts 10:44-47 While Peter yet spake these words, the Holy Ghost fell on all them which heard the word.
    45 And they of the circumcision which believed were <u>astonished</u>, *as many as came with Peter, because that on the Gentiles also was poured out the gift of the Holy Ghost.*
    46 For they heard them speak with tongues, and magnify God. Then answered Peter,

61

47 Can any man forbid water that these should not be baptized which have received the Holy Ghost as well as we?

You perhaps are going to read or hear some things in this lesson that you have never heard or read before; perhaps not. You won't be asked to take anything in this lesson at face value; check **everything** contained herein with the Word of God. The only thing that is asked of you is that you read or listen with an open heart and mind.

Skeptics have brought tape recorders into Pentecostal worship services and recorded messages in tongues (the gift of tongues in operation). When these same people tried to decode and translate these messages, they all came up with the same conclusion - there is no earthly language to match the language on the tape. We could have told them that before they bothered! *For he that speaketh in an {unknown} tongue speaketh not unto men, but unto God: for <u>no man understandeth {him}</u>; howbeit in the spirit he speaketh mysteries* (I Cor. 14:2).

This verse was written to people who had <u>already</u> received the Holy Ghost and who <u>already</u> had spoken in another tongue, a foreign language they had never learned, and naturally did not know. The language of the <u>Holy Ghost baptism</u> is a known tongue (language) and can be understood by someone somewhere on earth!

Let anyone bring a recording device and record someone speaking in another tongue (language) while receiving the Holy Ghost. They'll quickly learn that there is a matching language somewhere that is commonly spoken by the natives of that particular land! It is this power of God to cause a person to fluently speak a language that he has never learned and does not understand that completely baffles the unbeliever and makes him acknowledge that the Holy Ghost baptism is supernatural and of God!

Some of the things you are going to read and hear in this lesson might bruise your mind a little, but please keep an open mind as we pry truths from deep within the Word of God. Too many people are too satisfied to accept too much without thoroughly analyzing a subject for themselves, using the Bible as their plum line. Stand ten tongues-believers in a row, and you'd probably get ten varying opinions on the subject of tongues. This lesson gives scriptural evidence for every major point presented in it.

Because the gift of tongues is upgraded by some to a higher level than God intended, and relegated by others to a level far inferior to that which God intended, the subject of tongues is addressed in three different lessons: The previous lesson addressed the gifts of the Spirit, this lesson discusses <u>another</u> tongue (other tongues), and the <u>unknown</u> tongue is explained in the next lesson. It is intriguing to know that the subject of tongues was mentioned in Scripture long before they came.

*I.***PROPHECY SPOKE OF <u>AN</u> <u>OTHER</u> TONGUE (language).**
II.For precept must be upon precept, precept upon precept; line upon line, line upon line; here a little,

and there a little: ¹¹ *For with stammering lips and another tongue will he speak to this people.*¹²*To whom he said, This is the rest wherewith ye may cause the weary to rest; and this is the refreshing: yet they would not hear (Isaiah 28:10-12).*

Isaiah 28:10-12 foretold a coming event which was fulfilled first in the second chapter of the Book of Acts. Verse 11 of Isaiah 28 defines an event that God evidently intended to become truth. *For with stammering lips and <u>another</u> tongue will **he speak** to this people.* Think of it!

Isaiah was a Jewish prophet that preached to Jewish people. However, neither Isaiah nor the Jews to whom he prophesied understand that God would actually speak through Jews in tongues or languages foreign to them, called **<u>an</u> other tongue** - a language that they could not have learned or already known before receiving the Holy Ghost.

Isaiah declared in his prophecy that <u>an</u> other <u>tongue</u> (language) would be the instrument that God would use to speak to "this" people, indicating that the Jews were to be the first recipients of God's promise. The prophet had no idea, though, of <u>how</u> the Lord would speak to His people nor, that in doing so, that the prophecy would be fulfilled when His people received the Holy Ghost.

Joel, another Old Testament prophet, also prophesied of a gift that God would give His people.

And it shall come to pass afterward, that I will pour out my spirit upon all flesh; and your sons and your daughters shall prophesy, your old men shall dream dreams, your young men shall see visions:
*And also upon the servants and upon the handmaids in those days will I **pour out my spirit** (Joel 2:28, 29)*

Joel didn't realize that when he uttered the prophetic words, *I will pour out my spirit*, that he actually was foretelling something that would happen when people received the Holy Ghost. His prophecy was <u>fulfilled </u>in the Book of Acts: *And they were all filled with the Holy Ghost, and began to speak with other tongues, as the Spirit gave them utterance* (Acts 2:4). A subject of prime interest now is stated in the very next heading.

II. THE LANGUAGE OF THE HOLY GHOST BAPTISM.

From Acts 1:13-15, we learn several things. Verse 13 informs us that eleven disciples lived in an upper room in Jerusalem. Verse 14 tells us that women also tarried in the room with the disciples waiting for the promise of the Father, as were the disciples. Verse 15 states that there were 120 disciples that gathered together. This number apparently applied to men. The women appear to be an addition to the 120. But, whether the count applied to the men only or was a total number of all those present, at least 120 people were there when the Promise came. There is no break in Luke's narrative between chapters one and two. The very first word of chapter 2 is the conjunction "and." And what?

And they were <u>all </u>filled with the Holy Ghost, and began to speak with other tongues, as the Spirit *gave them utterance* (Acts 2:4).

The people in the Upper Room did exactly what the Prophet Isaiah said they would do. They spoke in **another** tongue, or **an other** tongue (language), and when <u>many</u> spoke in **an other** tongue (language), it became **other tongues** (other languages), the plural of <u>an other</u> tongue (language).

By "another" we are to understand that those who would and do receive the Holy Ghost will speak **an other** tongue or **language** they do not know. And when this happens it will be as the Spirit gives utterance, or the Spirit enables the receiver to speak.

Chapter 2 of the Book of Acts describes a phenomena that totally amazed all its spectators. We read these words in Acts 2:5: *And there were dwelling at Jerusalem Jews, devout men, out of every nation under heaven.*

In using the term "devout," Luke described as being very sincere the foreign Jews that witnessed the outpouring of the Holy Ghost on the 120. They had journeyed to Jerusalem from their homes in distant lands to keep the Feast of Passover, and they were still in Jerusalem fifty days later for the Feast of Pentecost. They were serious people, very God-fearing. They were interested in the things of God, or they wouldn't have gone to Jerusalem to observe the Passover in the first place. They could have done that at home, but they extended themselves to go to Israel, their religious home. As always, the Lord blessed them for being faithful. Notice Acts 2:6.

Now when this was noised abroad, the multitude came together, and were confounded, because that every man heard them <u>speak</u> in his <u>own</u> language.

The devout, foreign Jews, alongside countless others, went to see for themselves the amazing thing that had been advertised from mouth to mouth until it reached deep into Jerusalem. People fluently speaking in languages unknown to the speaker. To the foreign Jews that came to witness the followers of Jesus speaking languages they did not know, it was totally overwhelming. God's power shown by enabling the believers to speak in other languages totally **confounded** the multitude. Their complete amazement is borne out in Acts 2:7:

And they were all <u>amazed</u> and <u>marvelled</u>, saying one to another, Behold, are not <u>all</u> these which speak <u>Galilaeans</u>?

Only 14-16 languages are listed in Acts 2, but many more languages were spoken, apparently, since every foreigner heard them **speak in his own native language**, and every nation in the Roman Empire was represented in that multitude. (See Acts 2:5 again—*out of every nation under heaven.*)

The languages (other tongues, verse 4) spoken in the upper room were known, national, earthly languages - Acts 2:6. No interpreter was needed for each person in the multitude to understand his own native tongue or language. That amazing demonstration of the power of God prompted the question...

"*Are not all these Galilaeans*?" The people in the crowd wondered where and how this group of people could have learned and thus speak in so many different languages. Galilaeans would have known no more than two languages: Aramaic, their native tongue, or Greek, the language used by their conquerors, the Romans.

Those who stood around on the Day of Pentecost understood what the 120 Holy Ghost recipients were saying without need for an interpreter, because their native languages were spoken. The mere fact that these so-called "Galilaeans" spoke foreign languages that they could not have previously learned nor understand, proves beyond doubt that the **other** **tongues** spoken by them and **understood** by the foreign Jews present at Jerusalem, were earth and not heavenly tongues, or languages! Other tongues or another tongue is a foreign **and** **not** a heavenly language at all! But now, notice how God used the people's amazement to introduce a new truth. A natural question rang out from the multitude.

And how hear we every man in our own tongue, wherein we were born? (Acts 2:8)
It was the miraculous use of so many languages being spoken by people that did not know or understand them that enabled Peter to tell the multitude about God's promise from the Book of Joel. The following verses came from the mouth of Peter:

But this is that which was spoken by the prophet Joel:
And it shall come to pass in the last days, saith God, I will pour out of my Spirit upon all flesh: ... (Acts 2:16, 17)

These two verses tell us that it is the utterance (speaking) in **another** tongue (language) or **other** tongues (languages) that links Joel's prophecy in Joel 2:28,29 to the outpouring of the Holy Ghost on the Day of Pentecost when all the recipients of the Holy Ghost spoke in other languages as the Spirit enabled them to do so.

Joel's prophecy spoke of God "pouring out His Spirit." Isaiah's prophecy told of "another language." Peter linked Joel's prophecy of the outpouring of God's Spirit to speaking in tongues prophesied by Isaiah. Isaiah said, *"another tongue."* The tongue came when Joel's prophecy was fulfilled. The "other tongues" on the Day of Pentecost did not convict the Jews; Peter's preaching did that. The "tongues" brought amazement. Peter's preaching brought conviction. It's wonderful that other tongues did not cease in the first century, A.D. Let's continue.

II. OTHER TONGUES DIDN'T END WITH THE APOSTLES.

•   **Carefully consider the following verses:**

While Peter yet spake these words, the Holy Ghost fell on all them which heard the word.

And they of the circumcision which believed were astonished, as many as came with Peter, because that on the Gentiles also was poured out the gift of the Holy Ghost.

For they heard them speak with tongues, and magnify God. Then answered Peter,
Can any man forbid water that these should not be baptized <u>which have received the Holy Ghost as well as we</u>? (Acts 10:44-47)

These verses reveal the marvelous grace of God. The Jews had ingrained in their system that no one other than a Jew would ever be acceptable to God. The only avenue for hope to a non-Jew, in their opinion, was to become a proselyte Jew. Even the disciples and Apostles endorsed that attitude. What a tremendous shock to them all when God extended salvation to the Gentiles without embracing the Law of Moses.

The tenth chapter of Acts relates the tenacious resistance of Peter against receiving the Gentiles. Thankfully, he yielded to God by going and preaching to the house of Cornelius.

Cornelius was a centurion with one hundred soldiers under his command, yet he was such a prayer warrior that an angel appeared to him and gave him instructions to send for Peter. By the time Peter arrived, the whole house of Cornelius (family and servants, maybe soldiers, also) were gathered together. They anxiously zoned in on the Apostle's word, and ...*While Peter yet spake these words, the Holy Ghost fell on all them which heard the word* (Acts 10:44).

<u>Brethren, what shall we do?"</u>

IV. PETER ANSWERED THEIR QUESTION BY SAYING,

The effect that the Holy Ghost had on Cornelius and his house is described in Acts 10:44, 45: *And they of the circumcision which believed were astonished, as many as came with Peter, because that on the Gentiles also was poured out the gift of the Holy Ghost.*

For they heard them speak with tongues, and magnify God. - exactly the same way the people received the Holy Ghost on the Day of Pentecost in the second chapter of Acts. While rehearsing the event to his doubtful, ministering brethren, Peter affirmed in Acts 11:15 that Cornelius' house had received the Holy Ghost exactly the same way that the apostles and others had received it on the Day of Pentecost in Acts, chapter 2. That means that Cornelius and those with him spoke with **other tongues**. *And as I began to speak, the Holy Ghost fell on them, **as on us** <u>at the beginning</u>* (Peter's words in Acts 11:15).

Everyone can and <u>will</u> speak in another tongue (language), when they are filled with the Holy Ghost, and this **other tongue** will be a <u>foreign</u> <u>language</u> understood by someone somewhere on earth. Despite the myriad arguments against speaking in other tongues as the Spirit gives utterance, this wonderful experience is still available. The crowd in Acts, chapter two, that thronged around the people speaking in another language was mightily <u>convicted</u> by Peter's preaching. His preaching pierced their hearts to the point that they cried out, "...<u>Men and</u>

Repent, and be baptized every one of you in the name of Jesus Christ for the remission of sins, and ye shall receive the gift of the Holy Ghost. [39]For the promise is unto you, and to your children, and to all that are afar off, {even} as many as the Lord our God shall call (Acts 2:38, 39).

The Apostle just simply told them what he himself had already experienced. His Lord had baptized him, and he returned from the site of the Lord's ascension to Jerusalem to wait *"until ye be endued with power."* When that Power came, Peter and all the others in the Upper Room spoke in other tongues (languages) If Peter spoke in tongues (he did), was understood by foreigners (he was), and then promised the same experience to <u>everyone</u> (he did), then <u>everyone</u> will speak in **an other tongue** (foreign language) when they receive the Holy Ghost!

V. NOT <u>EVERYONE</u> WILL RECEIVE THE <u>GIFT</u> OF <u>TONGUES</u>, HOWEVER.

And that statement is addressed in the next lesson.

LESSON XII - THE {UNKNOWN} TONGUE

Lesson Focus: Our purpose in this lesson is to stress the supernatural aspect of tongues (the unknown tongue) in both its reception and in its use. This lesson will show that the gift of tongues is not resident, either - that is - the gift of tongues does not automatically come with the baptism of the Holy Ghost. It must be coveted earnestly, the same as any of the other 8 gifts of the Spirit. I Corinthians 12:31 advises concerning this: *But covet earnestly the best gifts:..*

Speaking in an {unknown} tongue is an operation of the Spirit. It is referred to by Paul as: *...I will pray with the spirit* (his own spirit praying in a language that he nor anyone else could know), *and I will pray with the understanding* (his own, everyday language) *also: I will sing with the spirit, and I will sing with the understanding also.* The Spirit language is not matched nor understood by anyone anywhere on earth: *for no man understandeth {him}* (I Corinthians 14:2). It is important that every Christian seek and receive the gift of tongues, because it is the only language the devil cannot understand. We need those private conversations with God!

This lesson will further attempt to explain the {unknown} tongue's operation and purpose in the church. We must emphasize the fact that all of I Corinthians was written to a church. Neither chapter 12 nor 14 explains the plan of salvation; the readers of this Epistle were already saved!

Scripture Selection: I Corinthians 14:2, 4-6, 12-19.

2 For he that speaketh in an {unknown} tongue speaketh not unto men, but unto God: for no man understandeth {him}; howbeit in the spirit he speaketh mysteries.

4 He that speaketh in an {unknown} tongue edifieth himself; but he that prophesieth edifieth the church.

5 I would that ye all spake with tongues, but rather that ye prophesied: for greater {is} he that prophesieth than he that speaketh with tongues, except he interpret, that the church may receive edifying.

6 Now, brethren, if I come unto you speaking with tongues, what shall I profit you, except I shall speak to you either by revelation, or by knowledge, or by prophesying, or by doctrine?

12 Even so ye, forasmuch as ye are zealous of spiritual {gifts}, seek that ye may excel to the edifying of the church.

13 Wherefore let him that speaketh in an {unknown} tongue pray that he may interpret.

14 For if I pray in an {unknown} tongue, my spirit prayeth, but my understanding is unfruitful.

15 What is it then? I will pray with the spirit, and I will pray with the understanding also: I will sing with the spirit, and I will sing with the understanding also.

16 Else when thou shalt bless with the spirit, how shall he that occupieth the room of the

unlearned say Amen at thy giving of thanks, seeing he understandeth not what thou sayest?
17 For thou verily givest thanks well, but the other is not edified.
18 I thank my God, I speak in tongues more than ye all:
1 9 Yet in the church I had rather speak five words with my understanding, that by {my voice}
I might teach others also, than ten thousand words in an {unknown} tongue.

Many people who have experienced tongues are taught that if they do not speak in tongues every day that they've out of touch with God. But is this true? How do those who demand this verify their teaching with Scripture? Personally, I enjoy that sweet communion in the spirit with God, even though my understanding is unfruitful. My spirit is uplifted during these times, and I know that something has been transacted in the spirit-realm that neither I nor the devil understands. And that is the beautiful part of it; the <u>devil</u> is completely bewildered when someone is speaking in tongues (the {unknown} tongue). He doesn't understand that language, and neither does anyone else! But I don't feel the least bit lost simply because I don't speak with tongues every day!

The gift of tongues (the unknown tongue) is but <u>one</u> of <u>nine</u> Spiritual gifts. Why would someone always desire to always speak in tongues when a supernatural manifestation is needed? A man dying of cancer would much rather see working of miracles than hear an unintelligible language. Someone up to his or her neck in frustration would love a word of wisdom rather than an {unknown} tongue, unless an interpretation follows the message.

As in **another tongue** or **other** tongues, the Spiritual gift of the **unknown** tongue can easily be mimicked and counterfeited. Most God-fearing Christians would definitely hesitate to even question "tongues." Miracles, on the other hand, are almost impossible to imitate (like a healing, for instance), so the insincere prey on others with their "tongues and interpretations."

There are two dangers facing people in trying to understand tongues - too much or too little emphasis being placed on this gift. Everyone needs to understand first of all that the gift of tongues (the <u>unknown</u> tongue of I Corinthians 14) is a gift of or by the Spirit in <u>addition</u> <u>to</u> the gift of the Spirit (the baptism or infilling of the Holy Ghost).

Every gift of the Spirit is important. We can conjecture only as to why Paul used the clause, *"Covet earnestly the best gifts,"* in I Corinthians 12:31. Perhaps the wording should have been, *"Covet earnestly the gifts best"* (for the church). Preceding this verse he wrote: *"And God hath set some in the church..."* He finished I Corinthians 13:31 with the expression, *"...and yet shew I unto you a more excellent way."* The Apostle did his best to assure that every gift of God be used for the edifying of the church and, thus, glorify God.

Some people resist the use of tongues in worship services; others feel that a service is incomplete without the operation of this gift. Sometimes this leads to fakery and outright hypocrisy by some when the genuine gift is not forthcoming. Why are tongues more important in a service than the working of miracles, faith, word of wisdom, etc.? The simple answer is, they aren't! But tongues are easier to simulate than some of the other gifts. This seems cruel and harsh, but it's fact, nonetheless.

Other tongues or **another** tongue (same thing) is the initial evidence of the baptism of the Holy Ghost. The **unknown** tongue is used in private or public worship and giving of thanks in the spirit. Both **another** tongue and the **unknown** tongue are both Spirit-given and Spirit-activated, and yet they are two distinctively different languages, and two different operations of the Spirit of God. The Holy Ghost evidence of **other** tongues is a known. earth language, understandable by someone somewhere on earth. The **unknown** tongue is just that - unknown, for *no man understandeth him* (I Corinthians 14:2). There is no earthly language to match this tongue! As in the last lesson, let's consider individually the verses in the Scripture Selection at the beginning of this lesson.

The Spiritual gift of tongues has definite identifications. We'll highlight some of these. Let's look at the first one now.

I.   THE {UNKNOWN} TONGUE

This tongue or language is mentioned first in Scripture in the following verse.

For he that speaketh in an {unknown} tongue speaketh not unto men, but unto God; for no man understandeth {him}; howbeit in the spirit he speaketh mysteries (I Corinthians 14:2).

The word "unknown" is bracketed and italicized in your Bible because the word did not appear in the manuscripts from which our Bible was translated. Its presence in the text is needed for clarity, however. {Unknown} is based on the expression *for no man understandeth him; howbeit in the spirit he speaketh mysteries*. This entire chapter emphasizes that this spirit language or tongue is completely **unknown** anywhere on earth. This is **so different** from **other** tongues or **another** tongue of the Book of Acts where **other tongues** were understood! So, what purpose does a language of the Spirit do for the person who is speaking? Scripture itself answers that question.

He that speaketh in an {unknown} tongue edifieth himself;... (I Corinthians 14:4)

The spiritual {unknown} tongue is given to edify(help, bless) the individual receiving this gift, who in turn will edify the church when this gift is exercised publicly.   Since this verse is addressing messages in tongues in the church, both the speaker and the church should be edified. If neither receives edification, then one of two things should be done, perhaps. First, allow the speaker to search his or her own spirit to check if the "tongues" message was genuine. If it's genuine, and it always should be, then the whole church should do some soul searching. Tongues are important, but they are not the only ministry of the Spirit to the Church. If no one is edified by the "message," it always is right to proceed with the worship service. It is erroneous to think that speaking with tongues is **always** the greatest ministry for a service. Notice...

*...for greater is he that prophesieth than he that speaketh with tongues, **except** he **interpret**, that the church may receive **edifying** (I Corinthians 14:5).*

In public worship, a message in tongues must be **interpreted** for the **church** to be edified. Only as we understand do we learn. If a message is given in a language that we do not understand, we are not benefitted, **unless** it's interpreted. When the Spirit is manifested in such a wondrous way in interpretation of an unknown language, a Holy presence awes every listener.

Tongues become **most important** in a service **when** they are **interpreted**. They deliver a message like "a breeze fresh from the throne of God!" People are always helped when they hear from God.

Please understand that the Apostle Paul did not caution anyone against tongues anywhere at any time. In fact, he endorsed this gift. Later in this lesson you will read where the Apostle said, "I thank God that I speak with tongues more than all of you." His purpose throughout this chapter was to give instructions on the proper use of tongues in the Church, and never a warning against allowing them into a worship service. He did warn about the misuse of tongues. Read on...

Now, brethren, if I come unto you speaking with tongues, what shall I profit you, except I shall speak to you either by revelation, or by knowledge, or by prophesying, or by doctrine? (I Corinthians 14:6).
Here's the same verse with inserts to clarify the meaning.

*Now, brethren, if I come unto you **speaking** with **tongues**, what shall I **profit** you, **except** I shall speak to you either by revelation* (interpretation), *or by knowledge* (something gained through education), *or by prophesying* (preaching under the anointing), *or by doctrine* (the printed Word).

Paul addressed the **church** in verse 6. The Apostle was concerned, and rightly so, that everything done during a church service should be done for edification (building up).

He left no doubt in anyone's mind that the {unknown} tongue could **not** be understood, and, therefore, needed interpretation by the Spirit in order to benefit anyone. Tongues (the unknown tongue) edify no one but the speaker unless they are interpreted. Everything done in a church service should be done for benefitting (edifying). Paul wrote the very same thing in the next verse.
*...seek that ye may **excel** to the **edifying** of the **church** (I Corinthians 14:6).*

Even **without** interpretation for a tongues' message in a worship service, the **speaker** still will be edified, yet Paul wrote: *..seek that ye may excel to the **edifying of the church**.* Since neither the **speaker** nor **anyone else** on earth could possibly understand what is spoken in an {unknown} tongue, Paul offered further advice in the next verse.
*Wherefore let him that speaketh in an {unknown} tongue pray that he may **interpret** (I Corinthians 14:13)*

During interpretation only do tongues become the **most** important ministry in a service. Without **interpretation,** tongues must **yield** to the other ministries so that the **church** may be **edified**. I Corinthians 14:28 informs us: *But if there be no **interpreter**, let him keep silence in the **church**...* This verse is purposely inserted here to add emphasis on interpretation, so please don't wrongly assume that once a person has spoken with tongues and there is no interpretation, that it would be wrong for a second message to go forth. Not so. The Apostle gave very specific instructions on this very thing later in this chapter.

The fact that Paul urged his readers to **pray** for an interpretation rather than <u>seek</u> an interpreter highlights the fact that the <u>unknown</u> tongue is indeed <u>unknown</u>. There is no <u>earthly</u> language to match it, so no interpreter could be found. Thus the need for <u>prayer</u> for <u>interpretation!</u>

Is this all to say that a person should simply maintain silence in a church service for fear that a message in tongues would transpire, and there would be no interpretation for it? No, no. Even if someone doesn't heed God's Spirit to provide an interpretation, the tongues' speaker will still be blessed. Paul wrote..

*For if I pray in an {unknown} tongue, my **spirit** prayeth, but my **understanding** is **unfruitful*** (I Corinthians 14:14).

The {unknown} tongue is "spirit" language, quite different from **another tongue** or **other tongues** that accompany the baptism of the Holy Ghost **and are** <u>known</u> earth languages!

Paul left no doubt that he understood **nothing** of what he said when he prayed in the **spirit** (in tongues). His spirit was uplifted, but his understanding was unfruitful. It is so evident that this gift of God is the link that binds the spirit of man with that of God. It is a communion between the two. On the other hand, **another tongue** or **other tongues** heard during a Holy Ghost baptism is an **earth language**, given by God to convince unbelieving, earthly beings!

Both the **{unknown} tongue** of I Corinthians and the **other tongues** of the Book of Acts are Spirit-given and Spirit-activated, but differ in the respect that **other tongues** can be understood naturally by someone since they are **spoken languages** used somewhere on earth, while the **{unknown} tongue** of I Corinthians 14 can **never** be <u>understood</u> naturally, *since no man understandeth him* (I Corinthians 14:2).
Paul strongly endorsed praying with tongues. Notice his wording in the next verse.

*What is it then? I will **pray** with the spirit, and I will **pray** with the **understanding**...*(I Corinthians 14:15)
The Apostle advised his readers to pray both in the **spirit** (tongues), and in the **understanding** (one's own language).

Having impressed their minds with the need for **interpretation** of tongues in **the church**, Paul also urged preaching and teaching in a known language. He also explained why <u>understanding</u> is so vital:

*Else when thou shalt bless with the **spirit**, how shall he that occupieth the room of the **unlearned** say **Amen** at **thy** giving of thanks, seeing he understandeth **not** what thou **sayest**?* (I Corinthians 14:16)

The Spiritual tongue (the **unknown tongue**) can **never** be understood except when God gives someone an interpretation for it.

Holy Ghost-filled people rejoice when someone speaks in tongues, even when there is no interpretation. Their spirits unite with the Spirit that enables a mortal to speak in a language that is not of this world. They never could say, "Amen," which is to say, "So be it!" if they don't understand what is being said, however. Far from condemning a tongues-message that is not interpreted, though, the Apostle commended anyone who will yield to the heeding of God's Spirit and utter a Spirit language. Regrettably, the loss incurred by a non-interpreted message is summed up in the following:

*For thou verily givest thanks well, but the **other** is **not** edified* (helped) (I Corinthians 14:17).

This verse states that even though a tongues-speaker does his job well, no one can understand him and, so cannot be edified or helped. This is good reason that **every** message in tongues be interpreted. Even the most spiritual of men can **not** understand the **{unknown} tongue** unless God reveals the interpretation of the message to him. It is a spirit language uttered by the Spirit of God.

Now comes the question: Did the Apostle Paul warn against or forbid the use of tongues in church? Well, here is Paul's statement on the subject.

I thank my God, I speak in tongues ({unknown} tongues) <u>more</u> *than ye all* (I Corinthians 14:18).

From the above Scripture, Paul clearly established the importance and necessity of speaking in tongues. *I thank my God, I speak in tongues <u>more</u> than ye all.* "Yes, by all means," the Apostle seems to be saying, "Allow the Spirit of God to commune with your spirit." Yes, yes, yes!" Tongues operate as the spirit's umbilical chord attached to the Spirit of God! Why would anyone **not** want this remarkable gift of the Spirit?

YET! Oh, oh! How did such a little word become so big all of a sudden? Considering all the other problems in the Corinthian Church that Paul had to warn, scold, threaten, and beg the people of that church to deal with, it's no big surprise that some of them also abused the use of tongues in church. And while the Apostle had just written that he spoke with tongues more than any of them did, tongues used during a church service are a different matter. Read on.

*Yet in the **church** I had rather speak five words with my understanding, <u>**that** by **{my voice}**</u> I might <u>**teach**</u> others also, than ten thousand words in an {unknown} tongue* (I Corinthians 14:10).

When Paul wrote {unknown} tongue in the above verse, he was referring to **any** language that was **unknown** to a congregation. **Unknown**, of course, also refers directly to the **unknown tongue.**

Now, read the **lie** instigated by the devil and mouthed by <u>unbelieving preachers</u> and <u>church members</u>:

>**"I had rather speak five words in my understanding in the <u>church</u> than <u>ten thousand words in an</u> unknown tongue."**

Paul **said no such thing**! He absolutely did not! This is so much like a story told of a ship Captain who despised his First Mate and wanted to get him dismissed. At the end of his watch, the Captain wrote the following entry in the logbook. "First Mate arrived for duty seemingly rational." After repeated, futile pleas from the First Mate to the Captain to change the language of the log entry, the First Mate retaliated. His entry in the log concerning the Captain was, "Captain reports for duty seemingly sober this morning." This is semantics in action - the use or misuse of words to project a message, commonly used in political campaigns. Now look at what Paul really wrote and meant.

When Paul wrote: *I had rather speak five words with my understanding...* , he <u>didn't stop</u>, but <u>continued</u>...*that by my voice I might **teach** others also...* How could anyone <u>teach</u> anybody <u>anything</u> unless the hearer **understood** what was being spoken? Paul stressed the importance of teaching in a service. Human beings can't be **taught** unless they understand what is being said.

II. LET'S SUM UP FOR NOW.

Throughout chapters 12 and 14 of I Corinthians, Paul endeavored to convince his readers, who were previously pagan worshipers of many gods, that there was only **one** God responsible for **nine** separate Spiritual gifts.

He emphasized the importance of **all** the gifts.

In chapter 14, he explained the proper operation of **one** of the gifts - **the gift of tongues** (unknown tongue).

He showed the difference in the languages spoken by Holy Ghost-recipients and that which is spoken by the spirit **after** the Holy Ghost is received. The **gift of tongues** is given to him that will **covet it earnestly**!

The Corinthians were famous for twisting things. Paul had more trouble with this church than with any other, apparently, and for this **we** can be most thankful. Due to the stubbornness and inconsistency of these people, Paul was forced to address **almost every subject** with which the modern-day church is faced. Thank God for the Corinthians!

Concerning tongues, he advised that it was only one of nine gifts, all important in the church of

God. In chapter 14, he showed a distinct difference between the Spirit-language (the {unknown} tongue) used by those endowed with the gift of **tongues** **after** having received the Holy Ghost and **other tongues** or **another tongue**. When they originally received the Holy Ghost, they spoke in **another tongue** or **other tongues**, which was a **foreign language** understood and spoken in some country.

Tongues, a gift of the Spirit, <u>is</u> **heavenly** language - the link between Holy Ghost-filled people's spirits and the Spirit of God. **Another tongue** or **other tongues** are <u>earth languages</u> ,which the Holy Ghost enables the receiver to **utter**.

Other Tongues or **Another Tongue** — Known Earthly Tongues.

{Unknown} Tongue — Spirit to Spirit Language.

LESSON XIII - USE OF TONGUES IN THE CHURCH

Lesson Focus: Speaking in tongues is often a misused gift. The {unknown} tongue is no more immune from God's government than any other gift of the Spirit. This lesson explains the proper use, limitations, and unexcelled horizons of this wondrous gift.

Scripture Selection: I Corinthians 14:4-7, 9, 13, 23, 26-29

4 He that speaketh in an {unknown} tongue edifieth himself; but he that prophesieth edifieth the church.

*5 I would that ye all spake with tongues, but rather that ye prophesied: for greater {is} he that prophesieth than he that speaketh with tongues, **except** he interpret, that the church may receive edifying.*

6 Now, brethren, if I come unto you speaking with tongues, what shall I profit you, except I shall speak to you either by revelation or by knowledge, or by prophesying, or by doctrine?

7 And even things without life giving sound, whether pipe or harp, except they give a distinction in the sounds, how shall it be known what is piped or harped?

9 So likewise ye, except ye utter by the tongue words easy to be understood, how shall it be known what is spoken? for ye shall speak into the air.

13 Wherefore let him that speaketh in an {unknown} tongue pray that he may interpret.

23 If therefore the whole church be come together into one place, and all speak with tongues, and there come in {those that are} unlearned, or unbelievers, will they not say that ye are mad?

26 How is it then, brethren? when ye come together, every one of you hath a psalm, hath a doctrine, hath a tongue, hath a revelation, hath an interpretation. Let all things be done unto edifying.

27 If any man speak in an {unknown} tongue, {let it be} by two, or at the most {by} three, and {that} by course; and let one interpret.

28 But if there be no interpreter, let him keep silence in the church; and let him speak to himself, and to God.

30 If {any thing} be revealed to another that sitteth by, let the first hold his peace.

In previous lessons, the chapter number and verse number is printed after each Scripture. This lesson gives a verse number only. Unless otherwise instructed, you will find the verse in I Corinthians, chapter fourteen.

The subject of tongues has been addressed quite at length in these lessons. Simply because a person doesn't understand a subject is not a good reason to ignore it. An electrician knows how electricity works, but he doesn't understand all the intricacies of electricity. That doesn't stop him from going to work. We will never know everything about the work of God, but we can know some of His works. Tongues is one of them.

May we never speak negatively when we teach about the **gift of tongues** (the unknown tongue's use **in** the **church**). Admittedly, this gift has been sorely abused. Since most of us know only **one** language, we don't know whether a tongues message is real or faked, except it be by the witness we feel in our own spirits. Too often, sadly, a church is not totally tuned in with the Spirit, so a great amount of fakery takes place over the years. This causes untold problems, and sometimes actual disaster. We need to stay in tune!

A second and almost as devastating a problem, is the **misuse** of genuine tongues. And this is due largely to a lack of teaching. A truly Spirit-filled Christian **never** has trouble accepting instruction given in the right manner. Hopefully, this lesson will show every reader how to make the **best** use of this marvelous gift — tongues **in the church**.

The {unknown} tongue, a gift of the Spirit, is given to an individual to profit (edify) the person receiving the gift. I Corinthians 12:7 states: *But the manifestation of the Spirit is given to every man to **profit** withal.* The blessing that the **church** receives from tongues is in addition to - that is, the church derives its blessing or edification from someone speaking in tongues **and** if there is an **interpretation** during a worship service.

Since tongues is an **individual** gift, its use in public worship must be governed. Just because the receiver is being overly blessed while speaking in tongues does not mean that everyone or anyone else will, too, **except** there be an **interpretation.** The one possessing the gift can and will be blessed (edified) at each instance of its use. Anyone hearing the exercise of tongues can only be blessed in **knowing** that the power of God is being displayed; his comprehension remains fruitless. And since the "assembling of yourselves together" (Hebrews 10:25) is to receive edification and instruction, everything must be **understood**, hence the need **always** for interpretation of tongues. Now read the first heading for this lesson.

I.TONGUES, (THE {UNKNOWN} TONGUE) BRING PROFIT.
He that speaketh in an {unknown} tongue edifieth himself; but he that prophesieth edifieth the church.

Only **he that speaketh** (with tongues) is profited (edified) unless his tongues' message to the church is interpreted. However, prophecy (preaching) **can** always be understood **without** interpretation so the **church** can always be edified or profited during prophecy. The gift is given to the speaker to profit withal (see I Corinthians 12:7). **Only** he that speaketh is profited **unless** there is an **interpretation** for the message. This is why Paul urged prophecy rather than tongues in a service, because prophecy or preaching would be in a **known** tongue (language), and everyone would understand and be profited. God's perfect and intentional will is that there be an **interpretation** for **every** message in tongues. This does **not** always happen, and the reason for this is addressed later in this lesson. So, we are to assume that it is always better to use prophecy rather than tongues in every service? No!

Walk with Me Through the Word

II.   PAUL WANTED EVERYONE TO SPEAK IN TONGUES.

But there's a right way and a wrong way to do almost anything, and the Apostle was anxious that a gift of God not be misused or abused. This is why he wrote the following:

*I would that ye **all** spake with **tongues**, but rather that ye prophesied: for greater {is} he that prophesieth than he that speaketh with tongues, **except** he interpret, **that the <u>church</u> may receive edifying** (verse 5).*

Paul said in verse 5: *I would that ye **all spake with tongues** <u>but</u>...,* and we <u>need</u> to understand the reason for the conjunction "but." He proceeded by urging them to prophesy rather than speak in tongues because prophecy is <u>always</u> **understood**, where messages in tongues are not, unless they be interpreted. When tongues **are interpreted** they become <u>**more important**</u> than <u>prophecy</u>!

We need to qualify his preference for prophecy over tongues by saying he had that preference **only** when there was <u>no</u> **interpretation** for tongues. Tongues become **more important** than prophecy, however, **when** they are interpreted.   When a message is given in tongues, God is doing the speaking. What could be more important than hearing straight from God?

III. HERE'S ANOTHER REASON THAT TONGUES ALWAYS NEED INTERPRETATION.

Now, brethren, if I come unto you speaking with tongues, what shall I profit you, except I shall speak to you either by revelation or by knowledge, or by prophesying, or by doctrine? (Verse 6)

Paul listed four ways that he could be understood by his listeners:
1. **Revelation:**   Interpretation of tongues, word of knowledge, word of wisdom, prophetical revelations.
2. **Knowledge:**   Things learned previously.
3. **Prophesying:** Preaching\teaching under the anointing of the Holy Ghost.
4. **Doctrine:**   Teaching from the **written Word**).

If <u>understanding</u> doesn't occur first, nothing else can happen. When Paul spoke of **revelation**, he probably was referring to **interpretation of tongues** more than anything else, since interpretation is a <u>revelation</u> gift. Of the four that he mentioned: revelation, knowledge, prophesying, and doctrine; **only one** is <u>not</u> a <u>revelation</u> gift. When he wrote *...how shall I profit you...?* he was trying to tell them that if they couldn't be understood when they spoke, they couldn't profit (or edify) anyone or anything. <u>Understanding</u> in listeners must occur before edification can become a reality.

<u>Understanding</u> is a prerequisite in more things than just the voice. Notice verse 7. *And even things without life giving sound, whether pipe or harp, except they give **a distinction** in the sounds, **how** shall it be known what is piped or harped?*

Surely, the Apostle must have been gazing ahead two thousand years into the last half of the twentieth century and into the twenty first century A.D. Music has become so cacophonous and disjointed that even the "musicians" and singers need sedatives to calm their nerves after a performance. Shame on people who allow themselves to be drawn into a whirlpool of frenzy! This spirit hasn't crept into today's churches -it' been **invited** and nurtured. How shall we be understood?

Paul explained the futility of preaching or teaching in an unknown language by a comparison to lifeless objects such as musical instruments that emit sounds. He contended that if these sounds don't make sense, then no results can be expected.

Since most of us possess knowledge of no more than one language, we could not understand tongues without an interpretation. We'd have no way of knowing whether we were being condemned, advised, asked or commanded. We hear **noises**, but we don't always **comprehend** them. **Understanding** precedes **comprehension**, which precedes **edification** or profit.

Though **understanding** and **comprehension** are basically the same word, a further explanation is here needed. If someone were to tell us in detail how to disassemble and reassemble a fine clock, could we do it? Probably not. Oh, yes, we could understand the instructions all right, but we wouldn't **comprehend** or gain the knowledge necessary to carry them out, so we would not be profited. We would have gained nothing but frustration from the instructions.

So likewise ye, except ye utter by the tongue words easy to be understood, how shall it be known what is spoken? for ye shall speak into the air (verse 9).

Unless lecturers speak on the same *intellectual* level that their listeners are on, they waste both their and their listeners' time, simply because they don't **speak the same language**!

A Master or Doctorate in theology or any other field is great so long as the possessor remembers that the knowledge that earned that degree is for his/her **own** edification or profit and not a tool to befuddle others. And on the subject of education, who is it to impress with the usage of words and language that are mystic, foreign, or beyond the educational orbit of those that hear? Which is more easily understood, ca. 1940 or about 1940? Both expressions deliver the same meaning, so why not use the simpler of the two? But back to the unknown tongue and its use in a message in tongues.

During a message in tongues, no one knows whether they're being chided, praised, advised, or comforted. Understanding, then, highlights the need for an interpretation.

Real or **simulated** tongues do **not** belong in a <u>sermon</u> or <u>lesson</u>. Speakers must talk their listeners' language or forget edification. Too often speakers "follow the leader," and since the other preacher or teacher mixes tongues with his message, it's **assumed** that it's right, and so others follow suit. Well, right it **ain't**! Unless a speaker is overcome with a full message in tongues that would deserve an interpretation, he should take great care that he doesn't allow his fervency in the Spirit to overcome his judgment and speak several phrases in an {unknown} tongue. Let's move on.

HERE'S GOD'S PERFECT PLAN FOR THE USE OF AND INTERPRETATION OF TONGUES.
Wherefore let him that speaketh in an {unknown} tongue pray that he may interpret (verse 13).
Anytime and **every time** a message is given in tongues, there **should** be an **interpretation**! Tongues **always** demand interpretation when given in a public worship service. Sometimes an interpretation does **not** follow, but that is **not** the fault of the Lord. **Non-interpreted messages** can not be allowed to continue endlessly in a service, however, and God has a ruling for that, which is addressed following verses 27-29.

AND HERE'S THE REASON WHY UNBELIEVERS ARE OFTEN CONFUSED.
If therefore the whole church be come together into one place, and all speak with tongues, and there come in {those that are} unlearned, or unbelievers, will they not say that ye are mad (crazy)? (verse 23)

This verse simply states that if **everyone** in the **church** speaks in tongues **at the same time**, that an outsider would think they were crazy. Everyone talking at the same time anywhere would just about drive anyone crazy! Many years ago (true story), a salesman's route caused him to visit a home every two weeks. Ma and Pa, the customers, liked to talk at the same time, and it didn't matter one whit that the other was talking. The tone and volume of both person's speech was about the same, and they each spoke vigorously, because they knew the salesman would stay for as little time as possible to finish his work. The poor salesman would look at one, then the other, smile and nod his head according to the expression on the particular speaker's face, and then turn to the other speaker and repeat his action. At the earliest moment possible, the salesman would make his exit from the home and shake his head. He had retained almost nothing of what either person had said, because they spoke at the same time.
Human brains are made that way. They can retain either-or, but seldom both.

Paul stressed the need for **understanding**. If we do not understand, we cannot be profited, edified, and neither can a sinner come under conviction until he understands.

In a prayer meeting where no instruction is intended for those assembled, there need be no individual interpretations, since each individual is communing in the spirit on an individual basis, and no **teaching** of others is intended.

Perhaps it was the exuberance felt by those gloriously delivered by the grace of God, who had lived their entire lifetimes bound by the demands of heathen worship, that caused the Corinthians to behave like feathers in a windstorm. But what's the excuse for today? Read the next verse, and then decide who Paul intended.

How is it then, brethren? when ye come together, every one of you hath a psalm, hath a doctrine, hath a tongue, hath a revelation, hath an interpretation. Let all things be done unto edifying (verse 26).

Paul did **not** condemn singing, teaching, and tongues, but he did scold wrong motivation. The Apostle asked, "Why do you <u>all</u> try to do the <u>same</u> thing at the <u>same</u> time <u>every</u> time you assemble for church?" Self-promotion and self-gratification too often are motives, when true worship needs to always be. Paul did not rule out **any** of the gifts of the Spirit; he simply was disgusted over their **misuse.** He gave his judgment on the matter when he finished the verse - *Let <u>all</u> things be done unto <u>edifying</u>."* Though the gifts are good, their use **can** be abused.

If any man speak in an {unknown} tongue, {let it be} by two, or at the most {by} three, and {that} by course; and let one interpret (verse 27).

Notice four things in this verse:
1. **Any man** (singular noun).
2, **By two**, or at the **most** by <u>three</u>. This signifies that **more than one person** may speak in tongues <u>during</u> a church service).
3. **By course** - meaning that each speaker must **take his turn**, and never speak simultaneously (at the same time).
4. **And let one interpret**. There should **always** be an interpretation. If God gives the message, He certainly can also give the interpretation that the church be **edified**.

Now for a recap of the four points:

Those that speak in tongues must do so **<u>singly</u>** and by **<u>course</u>.** There can never be more than **three** messages in tongues in any one service **<u>with</u>** or **<u>without</u>** an **interpretation.** Each speaker in tongues must **take his turn** and <u>never speak simultaneously</u> with someone else.

It **is** God's will that **every** message in tongues in a church service be interpreted. The God that gives the message is also quite capable of interpreting it. So, what should be done after three messages in tongues have been given in a worship service and still no interpretation?

*But if there be **no** interpreter, let him **keep silence** in the church; and let him speak to himself, and to God* (verse 28).

The absence of an interpretation for a message in tongues might be the fault of the **speaker** or of **someone** else not heeding the leading of the Spirit. But whatever the cause of **no** interpretation, the conclusion is the same - let him keep silence **in the church.**

He, or they who have spoken, do **not** have to refrain from speaking in tongues, **but** it must be done **silently** after three messages have been given publicly and not interpreted.

It is important to note that Paul advised about **edifying** the church, and after three non-interpreted messages, the church would still **not** be edified. The Apostle advised that after the third non-interpreted message in tongues that the speaker must *"...speak to himself, and to God."*

Considering from all that the Apostle had already written about the need for interpretation of tongues, it stands to reason that the Lord probably gives the interpretation for a message in tongues to more than one person. This conviction is borne out in the next verse:

*If {any thing} be **revealed** to another that sitteth by, let the first **hold** his peace* (verse 30).

A paraphrase of verse 30 would be: *"If anyone in the service receives the **interpretation** for the message in tongues, let the speaker **refrain** from **continuing** to speak."* Once a message is delivered, there would be no need for further speaking, and an interpretation surely wouldn't be given before a message is complete.

It would be rare for God to give **more** than **one** message in a single service. **If** a second or even a third person were to give a message in tongues, the messages would undoubtedly be identical to the first, if the first had not been interpreted.

Tongues are given for the purpose of **edifying** the church. **Once** a message is **received** by a congregation through interpretation, what further need for a **second** or even a **third** message? God is patient, but He is not endlessly patient. If a congregation is so out of tune that no interpretation is forthcoming at the end of a third message, then audible messages in the service must give way to other ministries. There would be no point in continuing tongues when no one understands and, thus, cannot be profited.

We must never be fearful of the move of God, but we also must always be careful that the flesh does not step in for self-promotion. And as alarming as it may seem, tongues-usage has been sorely abused. We need not feel condemned if we "question the spirits."

Now, let's address those who say, "I get so caught up in the spirit that I just couldn't quit." Nonsense! Pure nonsense! Here's why.

VI. THE SPIRIT OF THE PROPHET IS SUBJECT TO THE PROPHET.

Paul instructed one, two, or at the most **three** messages in tongues be given during any one service, and after that **silence** from tongues. No one can brush off his spiritual disobedience by the words, "Oh, I was just so moved by the Spirit that I couldn't help myself!" Wrong! There is **no** excuse for disobeying the Word of God. If a man can be anointed by the Holy Ghost to **utter** with tongues, then he must also obey when the Word of God says, "Hush! Speak to yourself and to God **in silence**." I Corinthians 14:32 states: *And the spirits of the prophets are subject to the prophets.*

Who said they **couldn't** shut up after a third non-interpreted message? Paul included I Corinthians 14:37 for just such a person: *If any man think himself to be a prophet, or spiritual, let him **acknowledge** that the **things that I write unto you are the commandments of the Lord**.* The Apostle may have seemed overly-bold, but he was right in insisting that his words were **commandments**, not suggestions.

If three messages go without interpretation, it's time to hush up and let the worship service move on. Wonderful things can happen when people operate according to God's Word.

Walk with Me Through the Word Questions Section

Questions for each chapter are included in this section for your use. The answers are at the back of the book after the chapter questions. Happy studying!

Lesson I: The Battle for Your Mind

1. What is the meaning of the word "doctrine"?
    A. That which is taught   B. That which is learned   C. Something you already know

2. Teaching hasn't been done...
    A. If the teacher doesn't hold your attention
    B. If you don't agree with something you're hearing or reading
    C. Until learning occurs

3. Of the 5 sensory perceptions of the human body, which 2 are most important in the learning process?
    A. Smell   B. Sight   C. Taste   D. Feeling   E. Hearing

4. People have roughly three times more optical (eye) nerves than audio (ear) nerves to the brain?
    A. True   B. False

5. 9 audio nerves connect the ears to the brain.
    A. True   B. False

6. "Give me the 26 letters of the alphabet and I'll control the world," was a statement supposedly made by _____.
    A. Joseph Lenin   B. Vladimir Mussolini   C. Vladimir Lenin

7. T.V. and computers are probably the 2 greatest tools available for spreading propaganda?
    A. True   B. False

8. Propaganda is something that is not necessarily true, yet is designed to change people's minds.
    A. True   B. False

9. Propaganda has almost completely reversed the political scene of the entire world in less than 60 years.
    A. True   B. False

10. More of the world's nations were democracies before...
    A. 1945   B. After 2,000

Lesson II: He's Alive

1. The Law of Moses was weak in that...
   A.   It offered no deliverance from sin
   B.   It didn't identify specific sins
   C.   Moses and not God actually wrote the Law

2. The Law of Moses was not designed to save but brought an awareness of sin.
   A.   True   B. False

3. Jesus Christ was buried in a borrowed tomb.
   A.   True   B. False

4. Because Jesus is alive, Paul was able to comfort his shipmates on a doomed boat.
   A.   True   B. False

5. Which Apostle was imprisoned on the island of Patmos?
   A.   James   B. John the Revelator   C. Simon Peter

6. On Mt. Moriah over 2,000 years before Christ, Abraham uttered prophecy about Jesus' crucifixion.
   A.   True   B. False

7. Josephus, a Jewish historian, wrote about the resurrection of Jesus Christ.
   A.   True   B. False

8. The resurrection of Jesus Christ is the _____ truth of Christianity.
   A.   Backbone   B. Minor   C. Only

9. Without the truth of Jesus' resurrection, Christianity would be no different from any other religion.
   A.   Maybe   B. Definitely

10. Jesus Himself moved the stone away from His tomb so He could get out.
    A.   True   B. False

Lesson IV: Repent

1. The word "repent" means to:
   A. Only be sorry for your sins
   B. Tell God you're sorry and change directions
   C. Confess and let it go at that

2. According to Matthew 4:17, we should repent because:
   A. The Kingdom of heaven is at hand
   B. We'll be sorry later in life that we didn't
   C. None of these

3. All biblical truths require how many witnesses?
   A. More than one   B. Don't need more than one   C. None of these

4. Matthew 18:16 and II Corinthians 13:1 are alike by stating that:
   A. Jesus' words were more important than Paul's
   B. They tell 2 different truths
   C. None of these

5. Repentance is what step toward salvation?
   A. First   B. Second   C. Neither

6. John the Baptist told his listeners they would miss heaven unless they repented.
   A. True   B. False

7. Repentance is a continual process.
   A. True   B. False

8. The Lord Jesus linked repentance to remission of sins in Luke 24:47?
   A. True   B. False

9. How many of the 7 churches of Asia did the Lord tell to repent?
   A. 5   B. 3   C. 7

10. It is very necessary for a person to maintain a repentant spirit on a daily basis.
    A. True   B. False

Lesson V: Is Water Baptism Necessary?

1. It is absolutely necessary to be baptized in water in order to be saved.
   A. True   B. False

2. Choose all the listed Scriptures that state that water baptism is necessary.
   A. Mark 16:16
   B. Acts 2:38
   C. 1 Peter 3:21
   D. Matthew 28:19

3. What does Mark 16:16 say: "That he that believeth and is baptized shall be...
   A. Have his sins forgiven
   B. Feel better for having believed
   C. Saved

4. 1 Peter 3:21 actually says that water baptism now saves us.
   A. True   B. False

5. Which 3 New Testament preachers that proclaimed that water baptism is necessary.
   A. Jesus Christ   B. Peter   C. Paul   D. Demas

6. No Scripture can be found in the New Testament where any preacher or teacher ever said that it was not necessary to be baptized in water.
   A. True   B. False

7. How many Scriptures must a person have to confirm a Bible truth?
   A. Only 1   B. None   C. 2 or 3

8. Did Jesus Christ Himself sanction water baptism?
   A. Yes   B. No

9. Pick the Scripture that links water baptism with the remission (removal) of sins.
   A. Mark 16:16   B. Matthew 28:19   C. Luke 34:47

10. Mark 16:16 tells us that baptism must be preceded by belief.
    A. True   B. False

Lesson VI: The Correct Bible Baptism

1. Give chapter and verse in the New Testament where a baptismal command is first given.
   A. Acts 2:38   B. Acts 10:46   C. Matthew 28:19

2. In Matt. 28:19, the words "Father, Son, Holy Ghost" are all **titles** and <u>not names</u> at all, so what did the disciples use when they baptized someone?
   A.   Title   B. Name   C. Neither

3. Every water baptism in the New Testament was done in what Name?
   A. Father
   B. Son
   C. Holy Ghost
   D. Jesus Christ, Lord Jesus Christ, Name of the Lord

4. Luke 24:47 tells us that remission (removal) of sins happens during baptism in His Name (Jesus Christ).
   A. True   B. False

5. The Great Commission is recorded (though not in the same words) in how many of the gospels?
   A. One   B. Two   C. Three

6. Matt. 28:19 told His disciples what to do, but He did not say, "Repeat my words."
   A. True   B. False

7. Jesus Christ gave the command to baptize in Matthew 28:19, and Peter obeyed that command in Acts 2:38 by baptizing in the Name of Jesus Christ.
   A. True   B. False

8. According to Hebrews 1:4, Jesus inherited His Name from His Father and nothing can be inherited that doesn't exist, so Jesus must possess the Name of His Father.
   A. True   B. False

9. If, as Hebrews 1:4 declares, that Jesus Christ inherited His Name from His Father, what then must be the Name of the Father?
   A. Father   B. Holy Ghost   C. Jesus

10. No Name is more exalted than the Name of Jesus Christ.
    A. True   B. False

11. Matthew 28:19, the Great Commission, is a command. Acts 2:38 is the fulfilling of that command.
    A. True   B. False

Lesson VII: You Must Be Born Again

1. Nicodemus was a religious leader of the Jews who became a disciple of Jesus?
   A. True   B. False

2. Give a definition of "born".
   A. To be brought into existence
   B. A natural birth
   C. A spiritual experience

3. Of what kind of seed are you born again.
   A. Different   B. Unnatural   C. Incorruptible

4. Which Scripture gives the correct answer for question three?
   A. Matthew 28:19   B. Mark 16:16   C. Neither

5. All of us must be born again to be saved. Pick 3 correct answers.
   A. We are spiritually dead
   B. All of us are sinners by birth but born again of the Spirit
   C. Everyone has sinned and, thus, must take on a new nature.
   D. There are not 3 good reasons to choose from

6. The reborn have power over sin.
   A. True   B. False

7. Anyone can be born again.
   A. True   B. False

8. When was Saul (Paul) the persecutor changed to Paul the apostle?
   A. Not known
   B. On the road to Damascus, Syria to persecute Christians there
   C. After he was jailed at Philippi

9. Who introduced Saul to the disciples at Jerusalem?
   A. Peter   B. Silas   C. Barnabas

10. Paul was just an ordinary preacher and really left nothing of spiritual value to the church after his conversion.
    A. True   B. False

Lesson VIII: Rest = The Holy Ghost

1. God used rest on the seventh day of creation to show or typify a greater rest in store for God's people of future generations.
   A. True   B. False

2. That true rest for the people of God today is the baptism of the Holy Ghost?
   A. True   B. False

3. The Holy Ghost baptism (the Rest that Isaiah prophesied about) is available still today to anyone who really wants it.
   A. True   B. False

4. The Holy Ghost baptism did not become available until the Day of Pentecost after Jesus was glorified and told his disciples to return to Jerusalem and wait for it.
   A. True   B. False

5. The promise of the Holy Ghost baptism will not cease until Jesus, the Perfect One, returns for His people.
   A. True   B. False

6. The Holy Ghost baptism always witnesses itself by enable the person receiving it to speak in an other tongue or foreign language that he or she could not know previously and still does not understand even after the experience.
   A. True   B. False

7. Which one of the following is wrong?
   A. God rested on the 7th day to show the coming of the Holy Ghost.
   B. A 7th-day Sabbath was commanded to show the coming of the Holy Ghost
   C. The H holy Ghost baptism was available throughout the Old Testament

8. Isaiah 28:11,12 clearly links God's Rest (the baptism of the Holy Ghost) to speaking in an other tongue or language.
   A. True   B. False

9. Isaiah 28:12 says that Israel's reaction to the outpouring of the Holy Ghost would be:
   A. They would not receive it
   B. They would realize their mistake in crucifying Jesus and repent as a nation
   C. All the world would be converted because of their repentance.

10. Peter tied the prophecy of the outpouring of God's Spirit in Joel 2:28 to Isaiah's prophecy of speaking in other tongues on the Day of Pentecost by his words "...that which ye see and hear is that..."
    A. True   B. False

Lesson IX: Rightly Dividing the Word

1. In studying the Word of God, we must first learn:
   A. Never study it alone
   B. Seek clergy advice before starting
   C. Learn how to study it

2. The three divisions of the New Testament are:
   A. Gospels
   B. Acts or Acts of the Apostles
   C. Epistles
   D. The Book of Revelation

3. The Gospels tells us of the birth, life, ministry, death, burial, and resurrection of Jesus Christ.
   A. True   B. False

4. The Gospels do not give the plan of salvation. No church founded.
   A. True   B. False

5. The Epistles give instructions to saved people on how to live, act, worship.
   A. True   B. False

6. The Epistles do not give instructions on how to be saved.
   A. True   B. False

7. Of the 3 divisions of the New Testament, only the Book of Acts tells us how to be saved, record actual incidents of baptisms in water and by the Spirit, and tell us these experiences are to all who are afar off.
   A. True   B. False

8. If a person wanted to find instructions on how to live, act, and worship, where would he look in God's Word for this information?
   A.   Acts   B. Epistle   C. The Gospels

9. If someone wanted to learn the life and teachings of Jesus, where would he look?
   A. The Epistles   B. Acts   C. The Gospels

10. If you want the full plan of salvation and see how people actually were born into the church of Jesus Christ, where only can you find this information?
    A.   Revelation   B. The Gospels   C. Acts

11. The thief on the cross still lived under the Old Testament Law because Jesus had not yet been glorified and ushered in the New Testament, so he actually was saved by the Law of Moses with Jesus as his substitute sacrifice:

    A.   True   B. False

Lesson X: Gifts of the Spirit

1. There are nine spiritual gifts. Select the alphabetical letter preceding wrong answers in the following.
    A. Wisdom
    B. Knowledge
    C. Faith
    D. Gifts of healing
    E. Gift of giving
    F. Working of Miracles
    G. Laying on of hands
    H. Prophecy
    I. Discernment of spirits
    J. Tongues
    K. Interpretation of tongues

2. Write the number of the group that matches alphabetical letter on the left

    Gifts of revelation.   A. _____   1. Faith, Miracles, Gifts of healing

    Gifts of power.   B. _____   2. Prophecy, Tongues, Interpretation

    Gifts of utterance   C. _____   3. Wisdom, Knowledge, Discernment

3. Paul needed to write to the Corinthians about the nine spiritual gifts because he needed:
    A. To combat polytheism   B. He wanted them to have more gifts of the Spirit

4. Paul said that every Christian would receive all 9 gifts of the Spirit?
    A. True   B. False

5. Paul said that everyone would receive the gift of tongues after receiving the Holy Ghost?
    A. True   B. False

6. Paul did not say that everyone would again speak with tongues after receiving the Holy Ghost?
    A. True   B. False

7. To forbid to speak in tongues is to forbid any and all of the other eight gifts.
    A. True   B. False

8. Paul said that tongues have already ceased.
    A. True   B. False

9. Which of the 9 spiritual gifts is the most important?
    A. They're all equal   B. It's a matter of debate C. The gift of tongues

10. Which of the 9 spiritual gifts is listed first?
    A. Wisdom   B. Tongues

Lesson XI: Other Tongues

1. When the scriptures talk of "a tongue, and other tongue, or other tongues" they are actually describing:
   A. A foreign language   B. A language no one can understand anywhere.

2. An other tongue or another tongue (same thing) was prophesied in:
   A. Joel 2:28   B. Acts 2:38   C. Isaiah 28:11

3. The Galileans in the Upper Room probably knew no more than 2 languages, yet they spoke in more than 10 languages when they received the Holy Ghost.
   A. True   B. False

4. God did not use tongues on the Day of Pentecost to convince the Jews?
   A. True   B. False

5. Whose powerful preaching did God use on the Day of Pentecost to "prick the Jews in their hearts"?
   A. True   B. False

6. Joel 2:28 prophesied the pouring out of God's Spirit; Isaiah 28:11 prophesied what would happen when this takes place?
   A. Nothing   B. People would speak in another language

7. In Acts 2:39, Peter promised that the baptism of the Holy Ghost was to those afar off. This was verified by when Cornelius spoke with tongues when he received the same experience in:
   A. Acts 10:46   B. Romans 3:15   C. Didn't happen

8. What verse in Acts 11 tells us that Cornelius and his household received the same experience that Apostles did on the Day of Pentecost?
   A. 5   B. 21   C. 15

9. What verse in Acts 2 informs us that the Holy Ghost experience was not confined to the apostles alone?
   A. 4   B. 10   C. 39

Lesson XII: The (Unknown) Tongue

1. For he that speaketh in an _____ tongue:
   A. Other tongues
   B. An unknown tongue speaketh not unto men, but unto God: for no man understandeth him; howbeit in the spirit he speaketh mysteries.

2. The word "unknown" is used concerning the unknown tongue (language) because there is no one on earth, not even the devil, who understands it.
   A. True   B. False

3. When a person speaks in tongues, he benefits (edifies) no one except himself unless his message is interpreted.
   A. True   B. False

4. Prophecy is never greater in the church as long as tongues are interpreted.
   A. True   B. False

5. Tongues are of little or no benefit to the church as a whole unless they are interpreted/
   A. True   B. False

6. While Paul was anxious that everyone in the church speak with tongues one at a time, he wanted the Corinthians to know that every tongues-message needed to be interpreted.
   A. True   B. False

7. 1 Cor. 14:14 tells us that when we pray in an unknown tongue that our spirit prays but we do not understand what we're saying.
   A. True   B. False

8. The key word of 1 Cor. 14:19 is teach.
   A. True   B. False

9. Paul said that he did what with tongues more than anyone else in the Corinthian church?
   A. Prayed   B. Sang   C. Spoke

10. Paul wanted everyone in the church to seek for a spiritual gift.
    A. True   B. False

Lesson XIII: Use of Tongues in The Church

1. He that speaks in an unknown tongue edifies:
   A. Himself   B. The whole Church

2. He that prophesies in the church benefits:
   A. Himself   B. The Church   C. Those praying

3. Paul wanted everyone to speak with tongues as long as they did it one by one.
   A. True   B. False

4. Tongues become more important than prophecy when they are interpreted.
   A. True   B. False

5. Paul wrote this epistle to:
   A. A Church, to saved people   B. To everyone   C. Sinners only

6. How many in the church did Paul want to speak in tongues?
   A. Everyone   B. No one

7. To avoid confusion, how many people could speak out loud in tongues in a single service?
   A. As many as 3   B. Everyone   C. no one

8. Could more than one person speak in tongues in a service at the same time?
   A. True   B. False

9. 1 Corinthians 14:28 informs us that no more than 3 people can give audible messages in tongues in a service, but further speaking with tongues can be done how?
   A. Silently   B. By going somewhere else C. Can't be done at all

10. A person can quit speaking in tongues in church once he or she has started and still obey the Spirit, according to:
    A. 1 Cor. 14:32
    B. B. 1 Cor. 10:46
    C. Must quit after the third person speaks

Walk With Me - Answers

Lesson 1: 1 – A, 2 – C, 3 – B, F, 4 – B, 5 – B, 6 – C, 7 – A, 8 – A, 9 – A, 10 – A

Lesson 2: 1 – A, 2 – A, 3 – A, 4 – A, 5 – B, 6 – A, 7 – A, 8 – A, 9 – B, 10 – B

Lesson 3: 1 – A, 2 – B, 3 – A, 4 – A, 5 – B, 6 – A, 7 – C, 8 – A, 9 – A, 10 - C

Lesson 4: 1 – A, 2 – A, 3 – A, 4 – B, 5 – A, 6 – A, 7 – A, 8 – A, 9 – A, 10 - A

Lesson 5: 1 – A, 2 – ALL, 3 – C, 4 – A, 5 – A, B, C, 6 – A, 7 – C, 8 – A, 9 – C, 10 - A

Lesson 6: 1 – C, 2 – B, 3 – D, 4 – A, 5 – C, 6 – A, 7 – A, 8 – A, 9 – C, 10 – A, 11 - A

Lesson 7: 1 – A, 2 – A, 3 – C, 4 – C, 5 – A, B, C, 6 – A, 7 – A, 8 – B, 9 – C, 10 - B

Lesson 8: 1 – A, 2 – A, 3 – A, 4 – A, 5 – A, 6 – A, 7 – C, 8 – A, 9 – A, 10 - A

Lesson 9: 1 – C, 2 – A, B, C, 3 – A, 4 – A, 5 – A, 6 – A, 7 – A, 8 – B, 9 – C, 10 – C, 11 - A

Lesson 10: 1 – E, G, 2 – (A-3) (B,1) (C-2), 3 – A, 4 – B, 5 – B, 6 – A, 7 – A, 8 – B, 9 – A, 10 - A

Lesson 11: 1 – A, 2 – C, 3 – A, 4 – A, 5 – C, 6 – B, 7 – A, 8 – C, 9 – C,

Lesson 12: 1 – B, 2 – A, 3 – A, 4 – A, 5 – B, 6 – A, 7 – A, 8 – A, 9 – C, 10 - A

Lesson 13: 1 – A, 2 – B, 3 – A, 4 – A, 5 – A, 6 – A, 7 – A, 8 – B, 9 – A, 10 - A

Made in the USA
Coppell, TX
21 March 2023

14544327R00059